"We all want the favor and bless
often don't know what his i
In *Favor*, Greg Gilbert revea
to all who have received his gi
your false labor for his favor.   challenge you
to see God's blessing in every aspect of your life, and live
accordingly."

—**Kyle Idleman**, author of *Grace is Greater*;
teaching pastor at Southeast Christian Church

"There is a better way to understand God's favor, and Greg
Gilbert gets it. In recent times, the prosperity people and
some charismatic characters have misunderstood and mis-
communicated God's blessings to his church. In *Favor*, you
will recognize what God's goodwill really looks like and
realize what it means in your life. If you want to sincerely
appreciate God's favor, read this book."

—**Jared C. Wilson**, author of *The Imperfect Disciple*
and *The Prodigal Church*

"In the wake of prosperity theology's perversion of the gospel, Greg Gilbert has provided a thoroughly biblical treat-
ment of what it means to live under God's favor and blessing.
As Gilbert reminds us, the gospel of Jesus Christ offers salvation from sin, not a platform for earthly prosperity. Christians are promised the riches of Christ, the gift of eternal
life, and the assurance of glory in the eternal presence of the
living God. Let this book shape your understanding of the
blessings of salvation and the benefit of union with Christ."

—**R. Albert Mohler Jr.**, president of Southern Baptist
Theological Seminary

"With unhelpful suggestions abounding as to what it means to
live in God's favor, this is a most timely book. Readability and
biblical accuracy characterize Greg Gilbert's writing. *Favor*
will not disappoint. I found it personally deeply encouraging."

—**William Taylor**, rector, St. Helen Bishopsgate, London

FAVOR

Finding Life at the Center
of God's Affection

GREG GILBERT

BakerBooks

a division of Baker Publishing Group
Grand Rapids, Michigan

Published by Baker Books
a division of Baker Publishing Group
P.O. Box 6287, Grand Rapids, MI 49516-6287
www.bakerbooks.com

Printed in the United States of America

Library of Congress Cataloging-in-Publication Data is on file at the Library of Congress, Washington, DC.

ISBN 978-0-8010-9321-0

17 18 19 20 21 22 23   7 6 5 4 3 2 1

To Jason, Matt, Ryan, and Seb.

Your friendship is a brilliant reminder to me
of God's favor to us in Christ.

And of course the steaks aren't bad either!

CONTENTS

INTRODUCTION

One of Those Days

I woke up to the sound of my phone's alarm ringing in my ears and promptly rolled over to hit the snooze button. Finally, two or three rounds of that later, I jumped out of bed and made my way into the kitchen, where my wife greeted me with a freshly brewed cup of coffee, a kiss on the cheek, and a cheery "good morning!" My sons were deep into their breakfasts and some last-minute homework before school, so I got the customary grunts of recognition out of them. My daughter, always happier than my sons to see me, looked up from her video on the iPad and put her arms out for a hug, which I gladly gave her. The dog, as he does every morning, pawed my leg and begged for food.

I had an early meeting that day, so I quickly took care of my morning routine and got dressed. There was a freshly ironed shirt in the closet, plenty of toothpaste, and a pair of clean socks waiting in the drawer (they didn't even have a hole in the toe!). The car started without any trouble, traffic was light, I made it to my appointment on time, and it turned out the person I was meeting simply wanted to spend some time encouraging me. Imagine! The two of us had a delicious breakfast together at one of the best places in the city, and then I drove from there to a church staff meeting, which also went off without a hitch. After that, I started tackling various projects and tasks. Some of them had been planned for a long time, and others just came up, as they have a tendency to do. But without fail, I nailed them all. It was as if projects completed themselves, problems dissolved, and tasks fell in front of me like dominoes without the slightest bit of difficulty. If this day was a basketball game, baby, I was Steph Curry!

Later that day, I found some time to go to the gym and had a great workout. I managed not to forget my gym shoes (which is a reason for celebration in itself), I hit every one of my goals for the day, and I felt all-around fantastic when it was over. When I got home, my daughter met me at the door with a hug, my sons grunted at me, the dog begged for food, and my wife welcomed me home and happily recounted her day. Then she pointed to the stack of mail on the table.

I walked over and began to sift through the pile, barely glancing at most of it before tossing it aside. There was the typical junk mail from the grocery store, a coupon from the pizza joint, and . . . something else too. Something completely unexpected. One envelope looked suspiciously official, and it was marked "Urgent." I tore it open and looked inside to find the biggest surprise of the day. My insurance company had made an error in billing and had sent me a wholly unexpected check for several hundred dollars! After my wife and

I celebrated this little victory for a moment, she called us all to the table, and we had a nice dinner together talking about the day, not yelling at the kids, and even managing (miraculously) not to spill anything. After that, the kids cleared the table without moaning or arguing, we played The Game of Life together (which I won handily, natch), and then we all eventually went to bed happy and healthy.

One of those days, right?

I know, I know. You're waiting for the catch. But really, there isn't one this time. It was a flat-out awesome day! Everything seemed to go exactly right. Work, family, finances, recreation—all of it—just seemed to be firing on all cylinders and moving in the right direction.

As I laid my head down on my pillow that night, I thanked God for everything that had happened during the day. I knew that all of it, every problem avoided and every good thing experienced, was a blessing from his hand and a kindness from his heart. In every detail of that day, it seemed as if heaven was smiling down on me. God was pouring out his blessings on me, and I was *dripping* with the favor of God.

Wasn't I?

Well, if so, then I'd seriously like to know what I did wrong in the seven hours I was sleeping that night, because apparently the favor of God shut off like a spigot during the night. The next day was nothing like the day before had been.

I woke up in a groggy fog with the first signs of a nasty cold taking shape and walked into the kitchen to find my family in the middle of a pre-school-day nuclear meltdown. I stumbled over to the coffeemaker, pushed the button, and turned to intervene in a "disagreement" between my two sons. Thirty seconds later, I turned to grab my morning joe only to realize I'd forgotten to put a mug under the dripper and had brewed an entire cup of coffee onto the counter. And, of course, all that was only just the beginning. I was late to my first appointment because I hit every red light in the city, I got nothing of importance done the rest of the day, and I had a full-blown cold by noon. Oh, and you remember that insurance check? Well, like a cherry on top of the day, my wife called me late in the afternoon to tell me the transmission in our car was shot, and it would cost about four times the amount of that check to get it fixed.

So much for the favor of God!

But hold on. Is that really how we should think about God's favor? If things are going well for us—we have plenty of money, our families are happy and healthy, things are breaking our way—then we can be confident that the favor of God is on us? And what if things *aren't* going so well for us? Should we then decide that God must be *disfavoring* us and start looking for what's clogging up the flow of blessings in our lives? These are all very real questions, aren't they? After all, if you're a Christian, it's actually very right and good that you should *want* to live in the light of God's love and favor. For that matter, it's also right and good that you should desire to *feel* his love and favor worked out in tangible, obvious ways in your life. But those good desires also seem to raise a boatload of problems. I mean, are we really supposed to try to determine how *much* God loves and favors us each day based on how well the day goes? What a crushing burden that would be to bear! After a long and terrible day, we would have to go to bed telling ourselves that it all happened because not even God likes us very much. That's awful! And what's more, are we really supposed to think

God's blessings and favor are dependent on something we do to earn them? Then we would have to drift off to sleep not only thinking that our day stunk because God doesn't like us but also feeling guilty over the realization that, one way or another, it was all our fault.

For a God who spends so much time in the Bible telling us that his love is steadfast and eternal and gracious and merciful, that whole way of thinking makes God sound awfully fickle. Doesn't it?

The Wrong Way to Think about God's Favor

As exhausting as all that sounds, sadly, it's exactly the idea of God's favor you'll be taught if you read any number of Christian books on the subject, or especially if you turn your television to certain channels. In fact, an entire cottage industry has grown up around the idea of "helping" people figure out how to "harness" or "release" the favor of God to make their lives better in various ways. If you listen and read carefully, the contours of this way of thinking are pretty easy to see.

For one thing, the favor of God is almost always defined as divine blessings being poured out in a person's life *so that good things start to happen to them right away.* Most of the time, those good things take the form of financial blessings— debt reduction, increased income, surprise cash, unexpected windfalls—and the evidence of God's favor in that person's life is that they are able to live a certain lifestyle. It's not just financial good, though, that's said to come with God's favor. A person will also have relational success with their spouse or children or friends, professional accomplishment at work, or even a new and unexpected personal charm that makes other people want to do kind things for them, even backing down and letting them have the best parking spot in the lot because somehow, in some way, they recognize that person is a child of the King. When those kinds of things are happening, the story goes, then the favor of God is all over you.

But it doesn't happen automatically, of course. If you want God's favor, you're told, you have to "access" it somehow. Like a bank vault that opens only if you know the combination, the favor of God is accessible only if you know how to crack the spiritual safe that keeps it locked up. How exactly you're supposed to do that varies from book to book and sermon to sermon. Sometimes the key is said to be a matter of keeping positive spiritual energy in your life by thinking good thoughts about yourself—a lightly baptized version of a doctrine of karma. Other times it's a matter of working up enough faith or praying the right kind of prayer. Believe that God will pour out his blessings on you, expect his best and ask for it in the right way, and you'll find it all happening. And if not, well, you must not be believing enough or asking in the right way. I've even heard some teachers say that the favor of God is like spiritual plumbing in our lives and that if we want God's generosity and blessings to keep flowing toward us, we have to keep the pipes clean and clear by being generous to others. God's favor is ours for the taking if only we can figure out how to tap it, access it, or release it—or maybe it's all of those at once.

One last characteristic of most popular thinking about God's favor is that it's almost exclusively bound to the here and now. Whether it's focused on financial, relational, professional, or personal success, the expectation seems to be that if God's favor is of any value at all, it needs to happen *now* . . . or at least soon. And if it's not evident in a person's life *now*, then pity that poor soul because God, for whatever set of reasons, must not be pleased with them.

This idea of God's favor reminds me of a video game I play sometimes with my kids called Mario Kart. If you've played it, then you know the key to the game is running your little car over as many "power-up" stars and mushrooms as possible, because when you do, wonderful things happen: you grow into a giant who can crush other drivers, or you become invincible and able to run them off the road, or you get a burst of speed . . . all for about ten seconds, and then it's gone. From what I can tell, that's painfully close to how too many people think about God's favor: it's a power-up mushroom for the circumstances of life. Do this, don't do that, pray this, rebuke that, and God will make you invincible for a few days, until either the power wears off or you screw up.

Surely There's More

Is that really it? Is that really what the Bible has to say about what it means to have God's favor—that it sits locked in a heavenly bank account, or clogged in our pipes, or hidden like a mushroom on the road of life and that if we can just access it, grab it, or capitalize on it, good stuff will happen to us for a while until it wears off?

Surely the favor of the God of the universe amounts to more than that.

Over the course of this book, I want to strike out on a journey of discovery with you—a spiritual and biblical quest to find some good, clear answers to those questions and maybe a few other ones too. In the process, I'm hoping and praying that this book will accomplish a few things in your mind and heart.

First, I hope that by the end of this book you'll see more clearly than ever that the favor of God is actually far bigger, better, and more glorious than you've ever imagined. To put it simply, I hope this book will make you desire God's favor in your life even more. Why? Because being favored by God is not just a matter of finding a good parking spot, or having a fat bank account, or even seeing your life filled with thriving relationships. It is infinitely more than that. In fact, if that's all you tend to think about when you think about living in the favor of God, then you're thinking way too small. You're thinking, as C. S. Lewis once put it, "like an ignorant child who wants to go on making mud pies in a slum because he cannot imagine what is meant by the offer of a holiday at the sea."[1] After reading this book, I hope the walls are blown out of your conception of what it means to be favored by God. I hope your eyes are wide and your heart is full at the sheer eternal magnitude of what God gives to those he favors. God's favor isn't about parking spots or money or houses or success or relational peace. It's about eternal blessings and riches that are beyond anything you could ever ask or imagine.

Second, I hope you'll see that the biblical idea of the favor of God is intimately connected to—and in fact *utterly dependent on*—Jesus Christ. One truly perplexing thing about most popular teaching about God's favor is that the entire system seems to run just fine without much reference to Jesus. Sure, there will almost always be a reference to him here or

there, but he seems far from *necessary* to the deal. I hope
you'll realize with crystal clarity by the end of this book
that to talk about the favor of God without talking about
Jesus actually makes no sense at all. Here's the thing: the
favor of God isn't some spiritual power-up that only a few
super-Christians attain, and it also is not the joy of finding
yourself in a higher tax bracket. The favor of God is actually
your most fundamental need, the thing you need more than
anything else in all the world. Why? Because the alternative
is to be *disfavored* by God, and that never turns out well.
My aim in this book is not to convince you that you should
want God to favor you. What I want is for you to see that you
actually *need* God to favor you. You *need* him to be pleased
with you, and it turns out there's only one person in all the
history of the world about whom God has said, "With this
one I am well pleased! He has won my favor!" (see Matt.
3:17; Mark 1:11; Luke 3:22). And that's Jesus. You'll need
to start with him.

I hope you can see the importance of all this. If you've
understood the favor of God as some higher level of spiritual
existence—a way to see financial, relational, or professional
success in your life—then you've been shortchanging it in
a massive way. You've probably also been running yourself
ragged trying to figure out the key to unlocking God's favor
and maybe even killing yourself with either the guilt or the
pride that comes from thinking the key dangles out there
somewhere like a golden ring for you to grasp as you speed by.

On the other hand, if you've *avoided* talking or thinking
about the favor of God because you think it's a phrase that
belongs to health-and-wealth prosperity preachers on television, then you've been ignoring a massive theme in the Bible's

teaching about the gospel of Jesus Christ, and also missing out on the wealth of joy that comes from realizing—right down to the depths of your heart—that you are a friend of God. The fact is, the favor of God is not some fringe biblical issue about money and how many head of cattle can fit on a thousand hills. It lies at the heart of the Christian gospel. God's favor is a spiritual and eternal necessity for us.

That leads me to my last and best prayer for you as you read this book. I hope it will cause you to worship God more fervently, to know his love and favor more deeply, to desire them more passionately, and to rest in them more fully. In turn, I hope these truths will give you courage and steadfastness in the fight, increase your confidence in God no matter what circumstances you're facing, and help you cut the roots of any shame or pride that might keep you from exulting in the reality of God's favor toward you. In short, I hope this book will expand your vision from this world to the next, explode the boundaries of your understanding of how much God loves you, and cause the breathtaking wonder of what God has done for you in Jesus to erupt in your heart.

After all, in the end, to be *favored* by God is to be *loved* by him—passionately, intimately, and *despite* our betrayal of him by our sin.

PART 1

THE FAVOR OF GOD AND HOW TO GET IT

1

What Is the Favor of God?

I almost went to prison when I was in college. It was a crisp fall day near the beginning of my junior year, and I'd decided to try to find a particular store in a city I was not at all familiar with. This was all a very big deal to me, mostly because of the car. For two years, I had been wheel-less, stuck on campus with nowhere to go and no way to get there. This year, though, for the very first time, my parents had decided to let me drive my car to campus. Something about a "surprising new maturity."

My car really wasn't all that much to look at, even though at the time *I* certainly thought it was. It was a 1991 Ford Probe hatchback, fire-engine red. Someone told me once that it was the "second nicest car" in my high school, a comment that somehow managed both to offend me and make me proud at the same time. Anyhow, after a two-year hiatus, my old friend the Probe and I were reunited, and now I'd driven her across the country to a new life. Like I said, I'd never been to this particular city before, and I'm not even sure GPS had been invented then, so it wasn't long before I found myself driving through a very sketchy area of a very unfamiliar town. And to make matters worse, I was running out of gas!

Now I should probably go ahead and admit right from the start that I was probably speeding. But who wouldn't be, right? At least a little? I mean, think about it—I was a college-age kid lost in a strange city, low on gas, and maybe starting to get a little worried. Under those circumstances, who *wouldn't* be going 57 in a 45 mph zone? To be honest, my first reaction when I saw the flashing red and blue lights behind me was not frustration or fear or anything negative at all. It was relief! Sure, I might get a ticket, but at least the officer would know where I could get some gas, and he could help me get back to the highway too.

For the first few minutes, it all went down like a routine traffic stop. I pulled over, the officer sat in his car for a minute or two, and then he made his way to my window. I explained the situation I was in, and he said, "Yeah, I'll give you directions. But first I need to see your license and registration." I handed them over, and then I waited. Just as you'd expect, the officer went back to his car to run my license and write up the ticket, none of which was in the least surprising . . . until I realized I'd been waiting on him to return for more than twenty minutes! That's when it slowly started to dawn on me that something had gone wrong. Terribly wrong.

This was not normal.

Eventually, the officer made his way back to my car and rapped on the window with one knuckle. I rolled it down, and he leaned in to get closer to me. "Son," he said, "what's your name? Your *real* name?" I'm sure you can see the problem here. It's never a good thing when a police officer asks you a question like that. I swore to him that my name was exactly what was printed on my driver's license, and he grunted. "Okay. So where'd you get this car?" *Where'd I get the car?* Now my head was spinning. What on *earth* did he think was happening here? The officer listened to my story, clearly not believing a word of it, leaned in closer, and said, "All right. I'll tell you what, my friend. You can either tell me the truth about where you got this car right now, or I can run you in for grand theft auto."

That's when the panic set in. Honestly, I don't remember much about the next few moments. I remember trying to convince this guy that I hadn't stolen my own car, and I remember being spectacularly unsuccessful at doing so. I also remember wondering what it was going to be like to call my parents from jail to tell them I'd been arrested for grand theft auto, and I remember quickly concluding it was going to be unpleasant.

And then I had a stroke of genius. All of a sudden, I remembered that in the glove compartment, tucked into the owner's manual, were two photographs a friend of mine had taken of me and the car on the day I'd bought it four years earlier. I asked the officer if I could rummage through the glove compartment, found the pictures, and handed them to him. "See? That's me," I pleaded, "and that's this car! And I look a lot younger . . . don't I?"

He looked at the photos for a few seconds, turned his eyes up at me, and nodded. "Okay, I'm not sure what's going on here, but I'm going to do you a favor, kid. I'm not going to arrest you. You're going to sit here while I go back to my car and figure this all out." It took the better part of an hour to untangle the whole thing, but eventually it became clear that there'd been some sort of bureaucratic mix-up. Though I had what looked like a valid registration on paper, somehow in the computers the car was registered to some other fellow entirely—and in a completely different state. So it looked to that officer as if I'd stolen the car and forged some documents to make it look legit.

I finally drove away that day a free man—and a grateful one. Why? Because that police officer could very well have decided to "figure this all out" *after* he arrested me, impounded my car, and dragged me down to the station. But for whatever set of reasons, he decided not to go that route. Maybe it was the photographs, or maybe it was the panic that set into my face and the tremble in my voice, but at some point his opinion of me changed. I went in his estimation from an auto thief to a scared but honest kid, and he decided to "do me a favor."

That's the thing about favor. It opens doors. It results in good. It changes things. And that's true in a *massive* way when it's *God* who decides to show it to you.

The favor of God is a common theme in Scripture. In the English Standard Version alone, for example, there are 142 occurrences of the word *favor*, and that's not even counting the dozens of times where the *idea* of God's favor is present even if the word is not. What's more, favor is a rich and multilayered idea in the Bible. A person can *find* favor, *earn* favor, *win* favor, *do* a favor, *ask* for favor, and *beg* favor. God shows favor to some and withholds it from others, and in fact, some of the most astonishing stories in the Bible show people being *surprised* to be shown God's favor.

So let's start with this. What exactly is favor? What does it mean when the Bible says someone has God's favor, and what result does that have in a person's life? I think we can say at least four things.

To Be Favored by God Is to Be Pleasing to Him

At its most basic, the idea of favoring someone means you are pleased with them, that they bring you joy and gladness. That idea shows up all over the Bible. Take this proverb, for example: "A servant who deals wisely has the king's favor, but his wrath falls on one who acts shamefully" (Prov. 14:35). You can see both sides of the equation here, can't you? If you act with wisdom, the king will be pleased with you; he will like you and have a good and generous attitude toward you. You will bring him joy. But if you act shamefully by embarrassing or defrauding him, the king will give you the opposite of favor. He'll be *dis*pleased with you, and his wrath will follow.

You can also see this idea very clearly in the story of Noah, because God's favoring of him is set in such stark contrast to God's attitude toward the rest of the world. Genesis 6 tells us that in those days humanity had become desperately wicked, so much so that "every intention of the thoughts of his heart was only evil continually" (v. 5). And because of that, far from being pleased with humans, the Lord actually *regretted* that he had made them. "It grieved him to his heart," the Bible says (v. 6). In other words, he was profoundly displeased with the sin and rebellion of human beings, and he determined to destroy them, to blot them out from the face of the earth. "I am sorry," he said, "that I have made them" (v. 7). This was disfavor to a new and frightening level. But then comes this wholly unexpected sentence: "But Noah found favor in the eyes of the LORD" (v. 8). In all the earth, there was only one person with whom God was pleased, one person toward whom he had a good and friendly attitude. That was Noah. He had God's favor; he brought God joy, and that made all the difference in the world to him.

Can you imagine what that must have felt like? The world was falling apart around him, literally being dismantled by the Creator, and yet Noah could rest secure, knowing that he and his family were free from God's wrath. When God looked at the world, his eyes flashed with fire because of its sin. But when he looked at Noah, they softened with love and joy. Even on that makeshift floating box in the middle of an endless sea of death, Noah didn't have a thing in the world to fear. The God of the universe was pleased with him.

So here's the first thing to realize: to be favored by God is to be pleasing to him, to bring him joy. That's really not a difficult concept, but it's hugely important because it helps us right off the bat to realize that when we talk about God's favor, we're not talking about some "extra" or "optional" power-up in the Christian life. We're literally talking about whether God likes us and therefore whether he'll show us kindness or wrath. Do you see? This is not a question of whether you'll live your best life now; it's a matter of whether you'll live at all. It's hard to imagine a more fundamental question than that.

Favor Is Intimate and Personal, Not Cold and Mechanical

One thing that strikes me about most popular teaching about God's favor is that it's all so cold and mechanical. Whether the image is karma or a vault or a reservoir or a plumbing system, it's all water and metal and gas—not heart and soul. That's terribly sad too, because we're talking, after all, about how God loves us and rejoices over us. Imagine if I thought of my love for my wife and kids the way so many think of God's love for us. "Honey, I want you to have my best; I really do. But you're going to need to access my favor by really expecting me to do good things for you and sincerely asking for it. And when I give you a little bit of my favor, you'll need to thank me. And be sure to really mean it when you do. Otherwise I'll lock up my blessings again until you get it right."

Thank goodness that's not how the Bible talks about God's favor. Instead, favor in the Bible is a deeply intimate and profoundly personal relationship between two people. There's a wonderful story in Exodus 33, for example, about Moses praying to God on behalf of the people of Israel just after God rescued them from slavery in Egypt. What Moses prays is for the Lord to show favor to the people by going with them as they head out into the wilderness. God finally agrees to Moses's request, but there's a fascinating detail in his answer that's often overlooked. Check it out: "This very thing that you have spoken I will do, for you have found favor in my sight, and I know you by name" (v. 17).

Did you see it? God's favor toward Moses means that God knows Moses by name. That's no cold, mechanical reservoir of blessing whose valves have to be monitored. That's a relationship between two people who know each other's names.

You've experienced this kind of thing in your own life, haven't you? Knowing someone by name is inherently intimate.

It speaks of friendship and ease. To be on a first-name basis with someone means you've dismantled the walls of formality and professionalism, and you now regard someone as a friend. In the same way, when you speak someone's name, you create a personal connection that can instantly communicate anything from anger to sympathy to excitement to joy. Just imagine the intimate joy that must have flooded Mary Magdalene's heart when she heard the risen Jesus say her name: "Mary" (John 20:16). In that instant, she *knew* him, and she knew that he knew her.

There's even more, though. Not only does favor mean knowing someone's name, but it's also bound up very tightly with seeing someone's eyes and face. Very often in the Bible, it's not just said that someone has "found favor" with someone else. It's said that they have found favor *in someone's sight*. Again, the idea is about as far from mechanical or transactional as it can possibly be. To show someone favor is to *look* at them with pleasure, to find joy in *seeing* them, to turn your *eyes* on them in friendship.

In fact, one of the main phrases used to convey the idea of favor is "to turn your face toward" someone. That's what King Jeroboam asked the prophet to do for him when God caused his hand to wither. "Entreat now the favor of the LORD your God!" he said (1 Kings 13:6). Literally, that means, "Beg for the face of the Lord your God!" In other words, ask God to turn *toward* me instead of away from me. Similarly, Jacob knew that Laban was no longer friendly toward him when he realized that, as the original language literally puts it in Genesis 31:2, Laban's "face" was no longer "toward him." In the Bible, to have God's face turned away from you was a disaster, the forerunner of death and destruction. Life and joy, on the other hand, came when he looked on you with a face full of favor.

I hope you can see the point here, because it's important for understanding why having the favor of God is such a good thing. It's not just that he begins to pour out some sort of divine gold dust on your life so that good things start happening to you and people start treating you with more respect. To be in God's favor means for him to turn his face toward you, to look on you with pleasure and even friendship. It is to be in a sweet and intimate relationship with the God of the universe.

If you're a Christian, have you ever stopped to consider that mind-blowing reality? The Creator of the cosmos, God himself, knows your name. He smiles when he looks at you. His face looks full into your own, not with anger or disappointment but with a radiant smile. Because you bring him joy. Oh, if we could only grasp that truth and drive it deep into the bedrock of our souls, it would change everything. Instead of facing life with fear and trembling, we'd walk through it with confidence, knowing that God himself rejoices over us. Instead of being puffed up with pride on our good days and beat down with guilt on our bad ones, we'd keep our eyes firmly locked on eternity—and on the smiling face of our God. And then how much more deeply we would understand what Moses was saying to the people of Israel when he blessed them like this:

> The LORD bless you and keep you;
> the LORD make his face to shine upon you
>   and be gracious to you;
> the LORD lift up his countenance upon you
>   and give you peace. (Num. 6:24–26)

To have God's face shine upon you, to see his countenance lifted up in joy when he looks at you—that's what it means to be favored by God.

Good Things Happen to You When You're Favored

As if all that weren't enough, the Bible also makes it very clear that good things *do* in fact happen to those who are favored. Genesis 39, for example, tells the story of how Joseph found favor in the sight of his master Potiphar. Because of the way Joseph handled his responsibilities and because God prospered those efforts, Potiphar was pleased with his new servant; Joseph found favor in his sight. And what was the result? Potiphar gave Joseph a promotion and made him "the overseer of his house" (v. 4). Sometime later, the same thing happened again when Joseph was in prison. He found favor in the sight of the prison keeper, and the result was that he was placed in charge of all the other prisoners.

Queen Esther is another example. When she was faced with the prospect of going uninvited into the king's presence—an act that very well might have gotten her killed—what saved her life was the fact that she found favor in the king's sight. Here's how the Bible describes the moment: "When the king saw Queen Esther standing in the court, she won favor in his sight, and he held out to Esther the golden scepter that was in his hand" (Esther 5:2). The king was pleased with her, and as a result, her life was spared.

That's the story again and again throughout the Bible. To have God's favor—to have his face turned toward you in love, to be his friend—brings life and joy and goodness. No, it's not always in the way we expect, and it's certainly not always according to our schedule. But it is, always, good.

The trouble here, of course, is that we often find ourselves so dazzled by what God's favor can *get* for us that we begin to value God's gifts more than we value friendship with God himself. We want the blessings, and therefore we can easily find ourselves giving little thought to the relationship that stands behind them. In fact, sometimes our hearts can be so selfish that if the blessings aren't flowing the way we think they should, we start wondering if pursuing God's favor is really worth the effort.

I have a friend who lives in another country. The two of us have been friends longer than either of us can remember. In fact, we probably met as infants in our church's nursery and then just grew up as the best of friends from then on. For the last decade or so, due to distance and expense, we haven't seen each other very often—maybe one or two days a year at most. But what fun those days are when they happen! We catch up on old news, tell stories, laugh, and just have a great time together. But imagine that on one of those occasions, my friend flies into my city, arrives at my home, and says, "Greg, you are my friend. I love you, and I cherish you as a friend. So here, take my credit card and go have a nice dinner at Chick-fil-A. I know you love it, and I want this to be a sign of my favor toward you."

Now as much as I love Chick-fil-A, there's no way I'd take my friend up on that offer. And I certainly wouldn't treat him like we're often taught to treat God: "Thank you, my friend. You are so good to me. But I also know that Chick-fil-A is not really your best for me. I don't want your plan B, friend; I want your plan A. So I'm trusting you right now to give me your best, to give me my best dinner now. I'm trusting you to send me to Ruth's Chris Steak House, because I know that your friends don't go hungry."

Ridiculous, isn't it? Yes, because the point of my relationship with my friend is not just for me to get a good dinner out of it. If that's all our friendship comes down to, it's not much of a friendship, after all. No, the real joy in our relationship lies in the time we spend together, the intimacy of friendship and fellowship we share. And if that's not there, then no gift in the world can make up for it. So really, why would we think it's any different with God? Why do so many books and preachers and television shows talk about the favor of God as if the point is what we can get out of it? Are there rewards and blessings that come from friendship with God? Yes, of course. But to think and act as if those blessings are the *point* really couldn't be more backward.

Do you know what the Bible holds out as the greatest of all God's gifts, the crown jewel of his favor? Believe it or not, it's God himself. It's not the things of this earth or the cattle on a thousand hills; it's not even pearly gates, golden streets, and a mansion in glory. The greatest of all the gifts God gives to those he favors is himself. That's why John, at the end of the book of Revelation—*after* he's described all the rewards of heaven and the new Jerusalem—comes to the greatest and most glorious reward of all: "They will see his face" (22:4).

Christian, when you think about heaven (you . . . do . . . think about heaven sometimes, don't you?), what do you most look forward to? When I was a kid, the streets of gold, fishing in the crystal sea, and a big mansion with a Dallas Cowboys flag on the front most excited me. Now that I've aged and taken on more responsibility, what excites me is the *rest* I'm promised! But really, what most excites me about eternity is none of those things. It's that, finally, I will look into the face of my Savior. Faith will turn to sight, and I will see him and be with him for eternity. You see? Ultimately, the joy of heaven is not about the gifts. It's about the Giver. As the old hymn says:

> The bride eyes not her garment,
>   but her dear Bridegroom's face;
> I will not gaze at glory,
>   but on my King of grace.
> Not at the crown he giveth,
>   but on his pierced hand;
> the Lamb is all the glory
>   of Immanuel's land.[1]

To Have God's Favor Is to Be Acceptable to Him

There's one more aspect of the Bible's teaching about God's favor that we haven't considered yet, and it's possibly the most important aspect of all. It's also perhaps the most . . . unsettling.

Here it is: to have God's favor is not just to be pleasing to him, nor is it merely to be his friend. It is to be *acceptable* to him. That word might come as something of a surprise to you, and it might even be a little troubling. Why? Because it implies that somehow we might *not* be acceptable to him. It leaves open the possibility that he might reject us and turn away from us in disfavor.

As unsettling as that thought is, though, it's exactly the truth. One of the most common words used in the Bible for "favor" is the Hebrew word *rason*. What's interesting about that word is that it is the one used in the book of Leviticus to describe a sacrifice that was acceptable to God. But here's the thing: not every animal brought to the temple as a sacrifice was acceptable. In fact, God was very specific about which animals would be worthy of his *rason*, his acceptance. Look how he describes an acceptable animal:

> If [an animal] is to be accepted for you it shall be a male without blemish, of the bulls or the sheep or the goats. You shall not offer anything that has a blemish, for it will not be acceptable for you. And when anyone offers a sacrifice of peace offerings to the LORD to fulfill a vow or as a freewill offering from the herd or from the flock, to be accepted it must be perfect; there shall be no blemish in it. (22:19–21)

If you stop and think about it, that description raises a terrifying realization. Yes, God's favor may be full and rich and intimate and life-giving when it comes, but it is not at all something to be taken for granted. God's favor is not something he just *gives* to anyone and everyone. The stark reality is that if we are to have God's favor, his friendship, his blessings and joy, we must first be acceptable to him. We have to be . . . worthy . . . of his favor.

Worthy? Of God's favor? If you're like me, maybe you just felt the earth open up under your feet and swallow you whole, especially since we've just spent time thinking about the wonder of living in the light and warmth of God's friendship. To be told now that we have to be *worthy* of all that is simply unimaginable. It's like sinking into a cold, dark ocean and watching the sun fade into nothingness. All of a sudden, receiving God's favor seems so impossible, so out of reach, so unattainable, so utterly hopeless. And yet, on almost every page of the Bible, God's favor is held out as something available to us, offered to us. So what's the deal? Is God torturing us—holding out something of infinite worth that we'll only ever be able to look at but never have? If we have to be worthy of it, is God's favor really attainable at all?

Well . . . sure it is. There's a very straightforward way to get it, and the Bible is clear about what that is. No, it's not the easy, do-it-yourself "keys" to which we so often retreat in order to make things easy on ourselves. We don't get God's favor simply by praying really fervently.

Or by believing with our whole hearts that God wants good things for us.

Or by expecting the best all the time.

Or by being generous with others in order to keep the pipes of God's generosity clear.

No. The Bible is clear about how we can attain God's favor: it has to be *earned*.

And good luck with that.

2

God's Favor—Is It Earned or Unearned?

Years ago, one of my best friends and I took a vacation to Spain. It was just a few months before I was going to be married, so this was what my friend insisted on calling (to my wife's continuing disgust) my "last hurrah." We did a ton of planning and settled pretty quickly on the general approach of the trip. We were going to rent a car and strike out on an epic ten-day road trip through sunny Spain. Beyond that, however, we didn't really know what we were going to do. In fact, right up to the moment we boarded the plane, we weren't sure if we were going to go east, which would have taken us to the beaches and party towns of Spain, or west to the mountains and ultimately through Portugal. In the end, about halfway through the flight, we decided to go west. Mountains, hiking, and history it was!

There are so many things I remember fondly about that trip. We explored cathedrals and nunneries, stayed a night in the famous Alhambra, watched swords being made in Toledo, hiked the Picos de Europa, and ate like kings. But I think the most memorable part of the trip was our stay right in the shadow of the Cathedral of Santiago de Compostela in northwestern Spain. The city of Santiago is stunningly beautiful, with ancient architecture surrounding quaint streets and the sounds and smells of the sea drifting through the air. And right at the very center of the city, overlooking a massive stone courtyard, is the cathedral itself. I'll never forget what it looked like the night we arrived—seagulls careening around its spires and the sun setting behind it in a brilliant sea-refracted crimson. I think I have never seen anything quite like it.

My friend and I wandered around the courtyard for a time, reading the tourist signs and brushing past the hushed crowds. Eventually, we walked up the front steps of the cathedral, and I saw something there that continues to this day to break my heart. There on the top step of the cathedral, carved through the centuries, were two deep knee prints worn into the stone from thousands and perhaps even millions of people bowing to kiss the feet of a statue of St. James as they arrived.

These days many people put their knees in those stone indentations mostly as a tourist experience, kneeling down and turning back with a goofy smile and jazz hands so someone can snap a picture. But historically speaking, the Cathedral of Santiago isn't a tourist stop at all. For well over a thousand years, it has been the terminus of a pilgrimage route called the Way of St. James. Millions of people have traveled that road through the centuries, sometimes for hundreds of miles and at great expense. For those people, the act of putting their knees in those granite indentations isn't an opportunity for a good photo op. It's a heartfelt, sometimes anguished cry for God to look down from heaven, recognize their great act of penance, and show them his favor.

Of course, that's not unique to Santiago de Compostela. That's how most of the world believes God's favor is to be had—by winning it, by earning it. From the woman in New York desperately trying to have an attitude of gratitude so God's favor will keep flowing into her life, to the man in Mecca marching around the great black Kaaba because this is what Allah requires of him, to the "good Christian" in Dallas going to church on Sunday in an effort to "balance out" what went wrong on Saturday—the human heart simply seems bent toward the belief that if God is going to show us favor, we're going to have to pay our dues one way or another.

Earned Favor

Why is that? Why do we so naturally gravitate toward the desire to pay our way through, to earn whatever it is that we have? I think it must have at least something to do with the fact that we simply like the feeling of accomplishment, of being able to take credit—one way or another—for what we have. That includes, of course, the favor of God. In a funny way, those knee prints on the step of the Cathedral of Santiago are monuments to human accomplishment as much as they are symbols of humility. After all, those pilgrims *made it*. Over hundreds of miles, through rain and danger and difficulty, they did it. They won. They accomplished.

They beat the Way of St. James. And maybe now God will take notice.

Does that sound familiar to you? It probably does; the desire for credit is a pretty universal phenomenon, I think. Maybe for you it doesn't have anything to do with stone knee prints, but we all have our trophies, don't we? It might be a job or a house, a car or a degree, or maybe even a literal trophy or plaque hanging on the wall that recognizes something extraordinary we've done. And that's the thing: one of the main reasons we cherish such things and even display them is so that other people will think well of us, so that they'll be pleased with us, so that they'll favor us. In fact, for most of us, the best and most desirable kind of favor we can imagine is a favor we have *earned*—a favor people give us because we well and truly *deserve* it.

Oh sure, we like it when good things come our way that we didn't strictly earn. It's exciting when we open up the mail to find that unexpected "correction" from the insurance company. It's fun to be the twelfth caller to the radio station and win tickets to a concert. But for most of us, when it comes to the main structure of our lives, we'd prefer not to live on the basis of other people's charity, much less their pity. We don't want people to show us favor and friendship because they have to or because they somehow think it's right to do so. We want them to favor us because *there's something in us worth favoring.*

Our desire to earn people's favor is, to a large degree, a natural and even a good impulse. So it's important to me as a father to teach my kids that they shouldn't live their lives looking for a free lunch. Instead, they should develop a good work ethic and earn both a living and a good standing with other people. In my own life, I want to do a good job at what I do so that people will see benefit in being a part of the church I pastor. In many ways, this desire to earn favor from others is a good and necessary part of being a well-rounded and productive person.

But there's another question: Does it work the same way with God? Is our relationship with him somehow based on earning his blessings? On the one hand, most evangelicals react immediately against that idea. "Of course not," they reply. "Salvation is by grace, not works." And, of course, that's exactly right. But on the other hand, another part of us always seems to want to assert that even if *salvation* is by grace not works, God's *favor* and *blessings* are something we can earn for ourselves. And that's when it starts. If we'll just treat people a certain way, we tell ourselves, or fill our minds with positive thoughts, or give money to this or that ministry, then God will respond and pour out his favor on us. If we'll just believe a little harder, pray a little more fervently, read the Bible a little more often, then God's pleasure will rain down like manna from heaven. It all sounds so simple, doesn't it? And so satisfying at the same time. After all, everyone loves a good business transaction: I give God this, and he gives me that. Tit for tat, as they say.

Now why is that? Why do we seem so convinced by—and even attracted to—the idea that God's favor has to be earned? I think there are probably many reasons. For one thing, many of us are quite convinced that, at least on our best days, we really can pull it off. We really can give God a reason to be pleased with us. We can *win* his favor. Have you ever felt like that? When things are going well, life is clicking, your mind is positive and full of gratitude, you did your quiet time, and you didn't yell at the kids and even managed to turn that one situation into a deep conversation about their hearts—then, yeah, you're feeling pretty good about yourself. And somehow we imagine God must be up in heaven giving us an approving nod and a slow clap from the throne. That's one reason we're so content trying to earn God's favor: it's because we think we can.

Beyond that, we also like the personal sense of accomplishment that winning God's favor brings. We like admiring our trophies, our knee prints in the stone. When we get right down to it, we are all such self-sufficient people, aren't we? And if we're honest, when it comes to the most important things in life, we usually don't like being given anything we didn't earn for ourselves. It rubs us the wrong way, steps on our pride, and elbows our self-sufficiency. Think about it: What if someone put their finger in your chest and told you that everything you have and everything you are were simply *given* to you, that you didn't deserve or earn or work for any of it, that it was all just *charity*? If you're anything like me, you'd be incensed. You'd spit and sputter and insist, "That's wrong! What I have I worked for." That's another reason the idea of earned favor is so compelling: we like to accomplish things; we like to win.

Another reason we want so desperately for God's favor to be earnable is because, frankly, we like to be applauded by others when we accomplish something. We don't want to keep our trophies in a closet. We want people to see them and celebrate them. So if it turns out that God's favor can be earned—if it can be paid for by a moral life or a pilgrimage or a way of thinking or a generous donation—then there's the possibility of applause for us in the end. And we like that very, very much.

Now at this point, you might very well be expecting me to make a decisive turn against the idea of earned favor, to say something like, "But that's not at all what the Bible says about our relationship with God!" But I can't do that. Why not? Because it turns out that this impulse we all have to try to earn God's favor, to win his pleasure, is . . . exactly . . . right.

That might be surprising, but it's true. In fact, the Bible couldn't be clearer that God's favor not only *can* be earned but actually *must* be earned. There's no other way to get it. Look carefully with me at this passage from Romans 2:

> [God] will render to each one according to his works: to those who by patience in well-doing seek for glory and honor and immortality, he will give eternal life; but for those who are self-seeking and do not obey the truth, but obey unrighteousness, there will be wrath and fury. There will be tribulation and distress for every human being who does evil, the Jew first and also the Greek, but glory and honor and peace for everyone who does good. (vv. 6–10)

Do you see what that's saying? Perhaps more clearly than anywhere else in the Bible, these New Testament verses are telling us the terms of our relationship with God. And they're stark. If you want eternal life, then persist in doing good; seek glory, honor, and immortality all the days of your life. If you want glory, honor, and peace from God, then do good— always and forever. That's it; that's the deal. But if you fail, if you are self-seeking, disobedient, and unrighteous, what you "win" is not eternal life but wrath and indignation.

It's a pretty simple system, isn't it? Do this and live; do that and die. If you want God's pleasure, *win* it. If you want his favor, *earn* it. It's not like this idea shows up in only one or two places in the Bible either (though that would be enough). It's *everywhere*, and it forms the fundamental basis of God's dealings with all of us as human beings. So in Psalm 62:12, David says, "You will render to a man according to his work." Proverbs 24:12 asks, "Will he not repay man according to his work?" In Jeremiah 17:10, God says, "I the LORD search the heart and test the mind, to give every man according to his ways, according to the fruit of his deeds." When God gave Adam and Eve their first instructions in the Garden of Eden, this was the deal: do these things and you will live, but if you violate this command, you will die. The New Testament says the same thing: "We must all appear before the judgment seat of Christ, so that each one may receive what is due for what he has done in the body, whether good or evil" (2 Cor. 5:10).

Don't let your mind race over this too quickly. It's all too easy to use our presuppositions as snow skis—a way to slide right over a truth that doesn't quite fit with the way we've always thought about it. What we've been talking about is one of those truths: God's favor is nothing less than his pleasure, his acceptance, his welcome. It is salvation. And it must be earned.

I'm not kidding. I'm not pulling your leg. And neither was the apostle Paul when he wrote Romans 2. He also wasn't kidding when he said a chapter later that one day each of us will stand before the judgment bar of God, that every mouth will be stopped, and that "the whole world will be held accountable to God" (Rom. 3:19). That's a terrifying image, and Paul *meant* it to be so. What exactly will it be like to stand before God, the One who sees our hearts and minds, who knows us perfectly and intimately? What will it look like when his eyes—which the prophet Habakkuk says are too pure even to look on evil—flash down at us and see our sin? What will it feel like for our mouths to be stopped, that is, for us to realize we have no excuse?

Unearned Favor

Of course, this is where most of us are counting on the situation to change dramatically. It's where you might even be expecting me to say something like, "But then what will it feel like to see God's face soften into love and kindness and for him to say, 'And yet my favor is given to you as a gift'?" It's even tempting to counter everything I've been saying by insisting that, actually, what the Bible teaches isn't *earned* favor at all but rather *unearned* favor. Maybe you've even heard a definition like that for the word *grace*—that it means "getting something we don't deserve" or "unmerited favor." I appreciate what definitions like that are trying to say; I really do. But I'm also afraid that, taken too far (which, let's be honest, is exactly where we tend to take most things), definitions like that actually wind up making God's grace and favor less glorious, less amazing, and therefore less valuable. They leave us thinking it's really no big deal at all for God to favor us and welcome us into his presence and that the blessings of eternity are so much candy to be handed out for free at the door of heaven. And that leads us to value them less.

Why? Because saying that grace is simply "getting something we don't deserve" or that it's "unmerited favor" isn't ultimately saying very much. It's like picking up the restaurant check for a perfect stranger. No, they don't exactly *deserve* that favor; they haven't *merited* it. But they haven't done anything *not* to deserve it either. You might say they're, well, neutral. Like Mephibosheth.

There's a wonderful story in 2 Samuel 9 about how David showed this kind of unearned favor to a man named Mephibosheth. Once he had secured the throne and deposed Saul, David called one of his advisers and asked if there was anyone from Saul's family to whom he could show kindness. "Yes," the adviser said, "there's a relative of Saul named Mephibosheth who is crippled in the feet." He couldn't walk, which meant he couldn't work either. David's actions toward Mephibosheth were a model of unearned favor. He sent servants to Mephibosheth's home, brought him back to the palace, and gave him lands and servants and a standing invitation to eat at the king's table. Mephibosheth hadn't done anything at all to merit or win or earn that royal favor; David just gave it to him.

But here's the thing: Mephibosheth also hadn't done anything to *lose* David's favor. He hadn't fought in any wars against David; he hadn't made a claim to David's throne; he hadn't committed sabotage or espionage or treason in any way. He was a blank slate in David's eyes, neither meriting his favor nor deserving his wrath. And David was kind to him. That's unearned favor.

If only we were in that same position in our relationship with God. If only we were at "neutral," having done nothing either to win or to lose God's favor and pleasure. If only Christianity really was about God giving us unearned favor. But it's not. Because we are not at neutral. No, our status is actually much, much worse than that.

We have *forfeited* God's favor entirely.

3

God's Favor Lost

Every year around Christmas, local news stations report on a phenomenon that breaks out spontaneously at various drive-thru restaurants around the nation. Called a Line of Sharing or a Line of Caring or sometimes a Pay It Forward Line, it goes like this: one festive and generous soul making their way through the drive-thru not only pays for their own triple-grande, double-pump, sugar-free, low-foam, no-whip, skinny vanilla mocha with a splash of coconut (or whatever) but also pays the bill for the person in the car behind them. When that blessed but unsuspecting soul arrives at the window, they're informed of the good news: the bill is paid, the latte is free, and there's nothing more to be done. That person, overcome with gratitude, then pays the favor forward to the person behind them by paying for *their* order, and the cycle repeats itself again and again until some ungrateful cad simply grins, says, "Cool!" and drives away.

I got stuck in a Pay It Forward Line a few years ago at my local Starbucks. I say "stuck" because for all the generosity and Christmas cheer and fa-la-la-la that's supposed to be involved, I look back on the experience with a certain amount of bitterness. It all started just like such things are supposed to. When I ordered my drink at the drive-thru, I was unaware that I'd already been swept up into a chain of joy and happiness, so it was a genuine surprise when I arrived at the window and the barista told me the person in front of me had paid for my coffee. I have to say, this brought me more happiness than a free cup of coffee really should. My heart swelled with gratitude, and I said, "Wow, that's awesome! You know what? Let me pay for the car behind me, and tell them I said Merry Christmas too!"

"Great!" the barista said. "Will do! Their bill is $27.92."

I honestly didn't know joy and happiness could drain so quickly. I considered a few strategies for a moment. Maybe I could pay for just *one* drink or put a down payment on the bill; maybe I could just laugh and drive away. But finally, through some combination of guilt, evangelistic necessity now that I'd brought Christmas into it, and a spirit of generosity genuinely reasserting itself, I paid the $27.92. I hope the guy in the car behind me enjoyed his drinks. I also hope he remembers my generosity as vividly as I obviously still do.

However you look at it, and whether you've been blessed or burned by them, Pay It Forward Lines are another example of unearned favor. After all, the person behind you hasn't done anything to earn your generosity. You aren't in their debt; they haven't performed some service for you; you don't owe them anything. On the other hand, they also haven't done anything to lose your favor. They haven't been rude to you; they haven't cut you off in traffic; there's no bad blood between you at all. They haven't earned your kindness, but neither have they forfeited it. You pay the bill as an act of pure, from neutral, unearned favor.

But let's flip the script just a little bit. What if you knew the person in the car behind you was your very worst enemy, someone who for years had unfairly and maliciously wronged you at every opportunity? Would you pay it forward to that person? Or to make it perhaps even a little sharper, would you *start* a Pay It Forward Line for that person? Whether you would or wouldn't isn't really the important thing now. The important thing is to see this: it's one thing to do something kind for someone as an act of unearned favor, when they haven't done anything either to deserve or to lose that favor. But it's an entirely different thing altogether to do something kind for someone who has set themselves against you in every way, who has in fact *forfeited* every right to your kindness and generosity. If we're honest, we'd probably admit that it would take something more than a little Christmas cheer to show that person kindness. It would take what we might call *gracious favor*.

Gracious Favor

Grace is an awe-inspiring word. In the Bible, it has a wide range of meaning, including mercy, compassion, pardon, and favor. It's not the kind of word that's used for unearned favor, though. Rather, it's the kind of word that has to sweep something else away to make room for itself—condemnation swept away by mercy, guilt swept away by compassion, sin swept away by salvation. And it turns out that *this* is the kind of favor we need from God—not merely *unearned* favor but *gracious* favor, favor that looks on us with pleasure and compassion and kindness and goodness not *because* of what we've done, or even for no particular reason, but *in spite of* what we've done.

If you're going to understand the value and preciousness of God's favor, you have to understand this first and above all: you do not deserve it. In fact, you deserve the opposite of it. You deserve to be condemned, to die, and to spend eternity under God's wrath, and no amount of being kind to other people or thinking positively or praying more fervently or going to church or making pilgrimages will ever be enough to change that verdict. It's as Paul said in Romans, "All have sinned . . . and the wages of sin is death" (3:23; 6:23).

I think the main reason so many Christians take the favor of God so lightly is because we think it's still available to us if we try hard enough. In other words, we fail to see just how completely and catastrophically we have forfeited it. You see, if your understanding of sin is that it's just a mistake or a misfire or even the violation of a duly enacted but not terribly important divine law, you'll never understand why it is so astonishing that God shows his favor to any of us at all. After all, even a child knows that it's good to be nice to people who aren't nice to you, so why should we be surprised when God does that for us? In fact, why shouldn't we *expect* God to do that? Well, here's why: it's because sin is not just a mistake or a misfire or a heavenly misdemeanor. It is rebellion and insurrection against the throne and crown and authority of God.

Sin Is Not a Mistake; It's Rebellion

You probably remember the story of Adam and Eve from the book of Genesis. Having completed the creation of the world in five days, God finally created human beings on the sixth day. The story contains an interesting little phrase, though, that is packed with meaning. It says that he created Adam and Eve "in the image of God" (see Gen. 1:26). Have you ever thought about what that phrase means? Many things could be said about both what it means and what it says about us as human beings. For example, perhaps it points to our ability to reason, or to create, or to relate to one another. All those things may be part of it. Whatever else it might mean, though, the phrase also points to a particular *role* Adam and Eve were supposed to play in the world—a *job* God was giving them to perform.

The idea and function of an "image" was well known to the first people who read the book of Genesis. Often when ancient kings would invade and conquer new territory, they would instruct their servants to identify the tallest, most visible mountain in the land and put on top of it a statue—or "image"—of themselves. Sometimes images like this were made of stone or wood, but sometimes they were made of more precious materials. You might remember from the Bible that Nebuchadnezzar of Babylon had his ninety-foot-tall image forged out of gold. Whatever the building material, the purpose of the image was unmistakable: it communicated to everyone in the land, to everyone who saw it on top of the mountain, that this land is ruled by this king.

Once you understand that, you can start to see a bit more clearly what God was doing when he created Adam and Eve in his image. He wanted them to perform a certain function. Even as they exercised dominion over the fish and the birds and the animals, even as they worked to subdue the earth under their feet, they were also to act as reflections—that is, images—of God's own rule over the world. In other words, their main job was to communicate to the universe by their very lives that this cosmos is ruled by God. Not coincidentally, that's also why God put the Tree of the Knowledge of Good and Evil in the center of the garden. As much as we might be tempted to think so, that tree wasn't just a nasty test to see what Adam and Eve would do with it. Much less was it a cruel temptation with which God was trying to lead them to sin. No, the tree had a definite purpose, beautiful in its own way. It was a reminder to Adam and Eve that the authority God had given them in the world was not ultimate, and it was not unbounded. It was derived and limited. There was an authority in heaven that was even higher than their own.

In the first days after creation, everything worked perfectly. The world and everything in it were beautiful—ordered and exquisite and wonderful, just as God intended. The waves crashed, the winds sang, and the trees swayed. Fish frolicked, birds soared, and animals roamed the earth. Creation rejoiced and worshiped. And like a skilled conductor leading an orchestra in a symphony, King Adam and Queen Eve led all of it in praise and worship to the High King, God the Creator, and enjoyed his unbroken pleasure and favor. No wonder God looked at all he had made and saw that it was very good.

And then it all came crashing down. One day Satan came to Adam and Eve, promising them that if they would just eat the fruit from the Tree of the Knowledge of Good and

Evil, life would get better for them. They could rise above their station. They could be "like God." Satan's strategy was ambitious. He wasn't just trying to get Adam and Eve to make a little mistake or to break a little divine regulation. Nor was he merely causing them to fail a nasty test God had set up for them. He was asking them to throw off the limits God had placed on their own authority, to declare independence from his rule.

He was asking them to join his rebellion against the High King.

And when they did, when they reached out their hands, ate the fruit, and set themselves in insurrection against God, they forfeited everything. Their relationship with him was severed, his pleasure turned to anger, and his favor and friendship turned to righteous wrath. He turned his face *away* from them.

Sin Is More Than a "Miss"

Sometimes our Sunday school definitions of biblical words can wind up confusing more than they clarify. Sadly, *sin* is one of those words. You may have heard someone explain that the Greek and Hebrew words behind our English word *sin* come originally from the realm of archery, and they mean "to miss" or "to make an error." The idea is that an archer, though trying very hard to hit the center of a target, misses the bull's-eye, sending their arrow flying out into the field beyond. No doubt that's a striking image, but it can be massively confusing if we apply it to the Bible's concept of sin. That's because our sin against God is not at all what that image of the disappointed archer would imply. Just like Adam and Eve, we are *not* in fact trying to hit the target God has set for us and just missing it by an inch. In fact, the truth is that in the deepest corners of our souls, we've decided not to aim at God's target at all but rather at his heart! We want him dead, gone, and out of our lives. We want his crown and his throne for ourselves so that *we* may rule and live as we please.

That ugly picture is the essence of sin. It's not a mistake, not a little white violation, not a miss or a shortcoming or a mere imperfection but a *revolution* against God and his authority over us. That's true of every sin, no matter how personal or small we may think it is. When we sin in anger, we are declaring that if only we could wear the crown, we'd make things work out better than God did. When we sin in pride, we are declaring that we ourselves are more worthy of honor and even worship than God is. When we chase after satisfaction and meaning and fulfillment in the things of this world, we declare that God and his beauty are not enough for us. When our hearts are filled with greed or lust or envy, we are declaring that we are discontent with the good gifts God the King has given us and that we want more, more, more! In all these things, we're doing far more than merely making a mistake. We're putting our finger in God's face—whether we intend to or not—and saying, "You are not worthy of my worship. You are not worthy to have authority over me, and I declare my independence from you!"

If that's true, then so is this: it is profoundly *right* and *good* for God to stand against us in our rebellion. After all, he is the Judge of all the earth, and as Psalm 97:2 says, "Righteousness and justice are the foundation of his throne." If he doesn't do what is right and just, in other words, the very foundation of his throne crumbles. And what is right and just when it comes to us and our sin?

To stand against us.

To pour out holy wrath against us.

To destroy us.

That's why we can't simply rest on a vague hope that God will understand we all make mistakes, or that he'll agree to overlook this or that shortcoming, or that he'll at least be reasonable enough to see we're not as bad as we *could* be. After all, a rebel is a rebel, and no king worth his salt extends his favor to those who have declared a revolution against him. God's withholding of his favor—his turning away from us in wrath—is wholly deserved and completely right and just.

But I'll Do Better!

Of course, this is the point at which we all start trying to fix the problem as quickly as possible. And without fail, the first reaction of the human heart to the realization that we are cut off from God's favor by sin is, "Okay, I'll do better! This time I'll change, and I'll obey God's law, and I'll earn his favor." I'll be honest; that's the first place my heart goes when I'm convicted of sin. Maybe yours goes there too—to a superhero-like determination to buckle down and just do better. But, of course, that's never going to work. In fact, the whole idea of working harder to obey God's law and win his favor is a lie that will cause us to wind up in nothing but despair.

Why despair? Because neither you nor I nor anyone else on the planet is capable—not even remotely so—of winning for ourselves the applause of heaven and the favor of God. Even on our best day, when we're killing it, we're not even close to winning that prize. Think about it with me for a moment. For one thing, we actually tend to get excited when we manage to obey one or two of God's commands, or meet one or two of his standards consistently. But what God demands if we're actually going to win his favor and earn his pleasure is *comprehensive* obedience. In other words, obedience in every detail. It's not enough to obey just *some* of his commands or even *most* of them. Even if we were to succeed in that, justice and righteousness would always be there demanding, "Nope, 99 percent isn't good enough. You broke *that* commandment, and that's enough to ruin you."

To make matters worse, winning God's favor would require not just comprehensive obedience to God's law and standards but *unbroken* obedience. So even if we could pull it together and obey everything from this moment for the rest of our lives, justice would still be there saying, "No, ten years ago, you disobeyed; you sinned. And so you lose." See, it's not enough to do good—or even to be perfect—from here on out. The sins we've already committed are still outstanding; they would still demand the loss of God's favor and the pouring out of his wrath even if we never committed any other wrong. Winning God's favor requires unbroken obedience, and the sad truth is we've already blown it.

Even worse, obedience to God isn't simply a matter of doing, saying, or even thinking all the right things all the time. It's a matter of doing all those things *from the heart*, with the right motives and for the right reasons. "Love the Lord your God with all your heart and with all your soul and with all your mind and with all your strength," Jesus said (Mark 12:30). That doesn't mean obeying with just some of your heart for some of the time. It means doing all the right things, with all your heart, all the time. Do you see how hopeless it is to decide you're going to buck up and win God's favor? Even if you could scrub your actions and your words and your thoughts completely clean from any disobedience to God, still justice would look into your heart and say, "No, that's still not good enough. Your motives are impure."

All this is what God's law demands of us if we're going to win his favor for ourselves. It's exactly what Paul meant in the passage we read earlier from Romans 2, when he said that God will give glory, honor, peace, and eternal life to "everyone who does good" (v. 10). Paul didn't mean that we need to be relatively good or mostly good or that we need to do a few good deeds. Even less did he mean that glory, honor, and peace will be ours if we just think more positively, or expect God to do great things, or keep the pipes of divine favor clear in our lives, or maintain an attitude of gratitude. No, he meant that if we're going to take a deep breath and try to win the favor of God, the standard we have to meet is to be good and to do good to the same degree that God himself is good. "Be perfect," Jesus said, "as your heavenly Father is perfect" (Matt. 5:48). Anything short of *that*, and we "fall short of the glory of God" (Rom. 3:23).

This Is Not a Game

I hope you can see why this is all so important to any discussion about God's favor. For one thing, we simply must stop thinking of the favor of God as a kind of carnival game that will net us some nice prizes if we figure out the trick to playing it well, or as a power-up status—like running over a mushroom in Mario Kart—that brings wealth and respect into our lives until we unfortunately lose it and drop back into the "normal mode" of life. It's not a game in which God is waiting to see if we'll be prayerful or faithful or generous or kind enough, and then he'll reward us by pouring out his favor on us in the form of a bunch of nice things and happenings. No, the favor of God is the most glorious and greatly-to-be-desired reality in the universe. In fact, it is not a *thing* at all. It is a relationship. It is God's taking pleasure in us, God's finding delight in us, and smiling on us, and turning his face toward us in love and acceptance. It is, most beautifully and staggeringly, for God the Almighty to say, "You are my friend." To speak or think of God's favor as anything less than that doesn't even begin to do justice to the glories of enjoying the favor of God.

And yet if we're going to understand even the basics of what the Bible says about the favor of God, we have to recognize that most of the books and sermons and YouTube videos out there about God's favor are simply wrong: *getting* the favor of God is not simple. It has nothing to do with our attitude of gratitude, nor with the pipes of grace being clogged up in our lives, nor with how fervently and sincerely we expect God to do good things for us today. God is not sitting in heaven longing to pour out riches in our lives if only we'll untie his hands by asking or believing or praying or whatever. He's not eagerly waiting on us to throw out our old wineskins and show him new ones so he can fill them up with the fine wine of favor. On the contrary, if there's anything the Bible makes clear to us about God's favor and its blessings, it is that they are completely and utterly and hopelessly out of our reach. We have forfeited them. We have rejected them. And we can neither do enough good nor erase enough bad to win them again.

As stunning as that truth is, once you grasp it fully, it has profound ramifications for how you think about yourself and your relationship with God. Most importantly, it's just deeply humbling. If you think of God's favor as something you can win by doing one thing or another, you will inevitably approach him with a sense of flippancy. Neither his holiness nor your sin will carry for you the proper weight. Your relationship with God will remain mostly a game that you can either win or lose. But when you start to realize that sin has irreparably broken your relationship with him—that you've forfeited his favor and deserve nothing but the death of a rebel—then you'll begin to approach him with the humility and solemnity he deserves. And that will change everything. Your prayers will be different as you stop demanding and expecting things from God and start humbly requesting them from the God of the universe. Your attitude toward other people will be different as you remember what you yourself deserve for your own faults and sin. Even your ability to weather the difficulties of life will increase, because you won't be hamstrung and frustrated by some hidden expectation that you somehow deserve better. The fact is you don't. And I don't. We are rebels against the Most High God, and we deserve to die. Let that reality sink in. Let that truth have its full effect in your heart, and you'll find it resets how you think about and approach every aspect of your life.

No One Is Righteous; No One

Do you remember that passage from Romans 2, the one in which Paul says you actually *can* win the favor of God if you just "do good"? We've already talked about what he means there—comprehensive, unbroken, all-the-way-from-the-heart good. But just a few verses later, Paul reveals how many people he expects to meet that standard and win God's favor. Look at what he says:

> None is righteous, no, not one; no one understands; no one seeks for God. All have turned aside; together they have become worthless; no one does good, not even one. (Rom. 3:10–12)

So here's the point so far: God's favor is not a game, and it is not some special gold-plated status that brings good things into our lives. It is the very friendship of God, and by our sin and rebellion against him—our repeated attempts to take the crown from him and rule ourselves—we have forfeited that favor. What's more, there's no way we're able to earn it back, and God cannot and will not simply suspend justice and grant us his favor anyway. No, his standard must be met. His law must be obeyed. Justice and righteousness must be honored and satisfied. His favor must be earned and won. But how? If we can't do these things ourselves, then how on earth will they ever happen?

Here's the answer: God's favor must be earned and won . . . *for us*. By someone else.

4

Jesus, the Winner of God's Favor

At 4:30 a.m. on May 29, 1953, a tall, lean beekeeper from New Zealand poked his head out of a tiny tent to check the weather. The wind had died down during the night, but the −17°F cold still bit at his face and stole his breath. Other than the wind and ice, the camp looked more or less like any other you might imagine. Canvas sheets flapped in the wind; metal pots and pans rested on the ground where they'd been left the night before, tinkling and clanking as they moved in the wind. Gear and equipment of various kinds lay strewn about. Really, the only difference between this camp and any other was its location. It was called Camp IX, and at 27,900 feet above sea level, it was the highest camp ever established in the history of mankind.

The beekeeper, whose name was Edmund Hillary, worked for the next two hours with his companion, Tenzing Norgay, checking their equipment and packing their gear. Then, at 6:30 a.m., the two men emerged from their tent and began their assault on the summit of Mount Everest, the highest peak on earth. For the next five hours, they picked their way through 1,100 vertical feet of ice, snow, and rock, always frightfully aware that one slip of an ice pick or one wrong step with a crampon would mean fatal disaster. Four hundred feet shy of the summit, Hillary became aware that the snow conditions had become "distinctly dangerous," as he put it, but "as no alternative route seemed available, we persisted in our strenuous and uncomfortable efforts to beat a trail up it." As he and Norgay made their way over what is known now as the Hillary Step and onto the final approach to the summit, Hillary finally saw it: all of a sudden, he wrote, "the ridge ahead, instead of monotonously rising, now dropped sharply away, and far below I could see the North Col and the Rongbuk Glacier. I looked upwards to see a narrow snow ridge running up to a snow summit. A few more whacks of the ice axe in the snow, and we stood on top."[1]

At 11:30 a.m. on May 29, 1953, Edmund Hillary became the only person in the history of mankind to stand on the top of Mount Everest. His companion, Tenzing Norgay, followed him almost immediately, but at least for a few moments, Hillary was alone in his accomplishment. He had done something no one in all of human history had done. He had summited Everest.

News of the ascent reached Great Britain on the day of Queen Elizabeth II's coronation, prompting the exultant newspaper headline the next morning: "ALL THIS AND EVEREST, TOO!" Hillary was world-famous before he even made it out of the Himalayan Mountains and back to the city of Kathmandu. Descending toward the city, he was met by a mail runner bearing an envelope addressed to "*Sir* Edmund Hillary, Knight of the British Empire." The newly crowned Elizabeth had knighted him before he had even made it off the mountain.

Part of what made Hillary's and Norgay's accomplishment so wonderful—and what so captured the world's imagination—is that so many others had tried and failed to summit the mountain. Members of an expedition in 1921 had been the first to discover what they thought might be a route to the top, but the climbers were poorly equipped for a serious attempt at the peak and so turned around and descended. Other attempts were made in 1922, 1933, 1936, and 1952, but none was successful. Time and time again, they all fell short of the summit. All of them, that is, except the beekeeper Edmund Hillary. He did what no one else had done. As another climber said of Hillary after his death in 2008, "He's iconic. I mean, he went to a place where no other man had gone before."[2]

The First, the Only

Truth be told, we don't actually know—for sure, anyway—if Hillary really did go where no other man had gone before. Some climbing experts think a man named George Mallory probably made it to the top of Everest in 1921 before he succumbed to the elements on the way back down. Others argue that it's very likely Nepalese Sherpas made it to the top long before the British even laid eyes on the mountain. Who knows? What we do know for sure is that Hillary didn't remain unique in his accomplishment for very long. Tenzing

Norgay set foot on the summit just a few seconds later, and thousands of climbers have summited Everest since then. Still, there's an enchanted moment between the first and the second when the first is also the only. And that's where our fascination naturally lies—in the moment when we can look at someone and our imaginations can thrill to think, at least for a moment, "*This* is the only person in the history of the world to have done this."

Edmund Hillary: the only one to summit Mount Everest
Ferdinand Magellan: the only one to sail around the world
Neil Armstrong: the only one to set foot on the moon
Roger Bannister: the only one to run a mile in under four minutes

And most important and astonishing of all . . .

Jesus: the only one to meet God's standard and earn his favor

I know, I know. That last one is not the kind of thing that makes it into the *Guinness Book of World Records*. You're not going to see a *National Geographic* special called "The Man Who Earned God's Favor." But if we had our priorities straight—if we were focusing on the most important things—Jesus's accomplishment of perfectly obeying God, completely meeting his standard, and actually winning his favor and earning his blessings would leave us more dumbfounded and astonished than any other accomplishment in the history of the universe.

A Life without Sin

Most Christians, when they spend time thinking about Jesus, tend to focus on his death or perhaps some of his parables and teachings. But have you ever considered what an incredible thing it really is that he lived his entire life without sinning? Like, ever? In any way whatsoever? Something like ten billion people have lived on this planet since the beginning of history, and out of all those, this man Jesus is the only one who managed to live a life that deserves anything from God other than death and condemnation. However you look at it, that's astonishing.

And yet that's exactly what those who knew him—his disciples, his family, his followers—said about him. According to John, "In him there is no sin" (1 John 3:5). The author of Hebrews said that even though he was tempted in every way imaginable, he met that temptation "without sin" (4:15). Paul said that he "knew no sin" (2 Cor. 5:21). And Peter put it about as plainly as it can be put: "He committed no sin" (1 Pet. 2:22).

I remember hearing that truth about Jesus throughout the years of my childhood, but I'm not sure it made sense to me until I began to realize what we saw in the last chapter—that sin is not just a matter of little wrong actions, thoughts, and words but rather a matter of the heart gone wrong, of the entire life bent in rebellion against the Creator, of deep-running deposits of sin that mar the very depths of the soul. When you start to see sin like that, in all its rebellious ugliness, Jesus's accomplishment of living a life with no sin whatsoever will leave your jaw on the ground.

Stop reading for three seconds. Go! (Ticktock, ticktock, ticktock.) There. I think I did it. I *think* I just managed right there—for about three seconds—not to sin in word, deed, or thought. I didn't say anything at all, so I'm pretty sure I didn't sin in word. Given that I tried to be as still as possible, I also think I managed not to *do* anything particularly sinful either. I even tried my best to clear my mind of thoughts (you can do it if you try really hard, at least for three seconds), so I don't think I sinned in those three seconds even in my mind. Not bad, right? And honestly, if that's all being "without sin" entails, I can actually get my mind around the idea that Jesus might have done it. After all, if I can do it for three seconds, it's at least conceivable to me that Jesus could have done it for thirty-three years. That's not an insane thought to me.

But then I remember that sin isn't just about words, deeds, and thoughts. It's also about the motivations of the heart, and *that's* when I stand in slack-jawed awe at what Jesus did, because even if I didn't sin with my speech, actions, or mind, I can tell you right now that my motivations weren't pure and godly even for those three seconds. I'm not going to deny that I was at least a little bit proud of myself for not sinning even for that long. And I certainly wasn't doing that little exercise in order to love the Lord my God with all my heart, soul, mind, and strength. If I'm honest, I was doing it to see if *I* could do it. See? That's what's so astounding about the fact that Jesus was sinless. He did everything right. He said everything right. He thought everything right. And he did it all—all the time—for all the right reasons and out of a heart motivated perfectly by love for God and a desire for his glory. Astounding.

Do you remember what we said in the last chapter about the standard God sets for us? Our obedience to and love for him have to be comprehensive, unbroken, and from the heart. That's what Jesus did. He obeyed God's law without fail, without pause, and with a completely undivided heart.

And here's why that's so important: when he did that, he earned—he merited, he won—God's favor.

There Is One Who Does Good

When Jesus was baptized in the Jordan River by John the Baptist, God declared that Jesus had won his favor. As Jesus came up out of the water, the biblical writers tell us, the Holy Spirit came down like a dove to rest on him, and a voice from heaven said, "This is my beloved Son, with whom I am well pleased" (Matt. 3:17). The words *well pleased* actually translate the same words that in the Old Testament mean "I delight in him" and "I am pleased with him." In other words, God declared over Jesus, "This one has my favor!"

Now if you understand what we've been talking about since the beginning of this book, if you understand how desperately you need the favor of God, then your heart should thrill to hear those words: "I am well pleased with this one. I delight in him. He is acceptable to me. He has my favor." And understand this too: that's more than just a personal opinion from God about Jesus. It is a *verdict*. It's a judicial declaration from the throne of the cosmos that for the first and only time in human history, someone has finally done it. Someone has met God's standard, accomplished what he requires, and earned his favor. It's the verdict we all so desperately need and yet have all so catastrophically forfeited: "You are acceptable; you are righteous; you are pleasing to me."

To put it another way, Jesus met the terms Paul laid out in that frightening passage in Romans 2. He sought all the days of his life for glory and honor and immortality. He did good—not just relatively or in comparison with others but *perfect* good. Indeed, if Paul rewrote the verdict of Romans 3:10–12 about Jesus, it would read like a celebration:

> This one is righteous, yes, this one; he understands; he seeks for God. All others have turned aside, but he has finished it; together *they* have become worthless, but *he* has become all in all! There is one who does good, yes, only . . . one!

Not Just Favor but Favor's Reward

Revelation shows us the angels in heaven recognizing what Jesus did through his sinless life. "Worthy are you!" they cry to Jesus. "Worthy is the Lamb!" (5:9, 12). He did what was required, and therefore he won God's favor. And yet there's something more as well.

The angels also say that because he won God's favor, Jesus is also worthy of all the rewards of heaven and eternity. Look at what they say: "Worthy is the Lamb . . . to receive power and wealth and wisdom and might and honor and glory and blessing! . . . To him who sits on the throne and to the Lamb be blessing and honor and glory and might forever and ever!" (Rev. 5:12–13). In winning God's favor, Jesus also won all the blessings that come with it. He is the only person in history who could say, by right, "I have earned God's blessing, and his favor is all over me!" (How ridiculous it is, in light of that, for anyone else—you, me, television preachers—to try to make the same claim.)

Stop and notice one crucial thing: even though Jesus earned God's pleasure, even though he had God's favor and all the blessings that attend it, *that reality did not translate into material blessings.* Jesus was not rich. Foxes have holes in the ground in which to sleep, and birds have nests, but he himself had nowhere to lay his head (Matt. 8:20). Nor were his earthly relationships smooth and free of trouble; his own family thought he was crazy, and one of his twelve best friends betrayed him. He didn't enjoy a strange new respect from those around him either; the leaders of the people hated him and mocked him even when he was dying. And he certainly didn't live the good life or the easy life. What an astonishing thing to realize! For the one man in history who actually managed to earn God's favor, life was a cauldron of hardship, betrayal, rejection, torture, and death.

If nothing else, those facts alone should disabuse us of *any* idea that God's favor is about material blessings in this age. What Jesus the Well-Pleasing One received from God were blessings to be sure, but blessings of *infinitely* more value and importance than the ones we spend so much time hoping and wishing for. Let's think about what those blessings were.

For one thing, Jesus received the kingdom—the crown and throne that God exalted over every other power in the universe. "All authority in heaven and on earth has been given to me," he said (Matt. 28:18). "Worthy are you . . . to receive glory and honor and power!" the angels said (Rev. 4:11). For Jesus the Well-Pleasing One, God's favor didn't mean he would have a nice house. It meant he would have a throne. Not only so, it also meant he would live forever in the joy and happiness and glory of his Father. "This is my beloved Son!" the voice from heaven said (Matt. 3:17). "To him who sits on the throne and to the Lamb," the angels cried, "be blessing and honor and glory and might forever and ever!" (Rev. 5:13). Jesus's reward for earning God's favor wasn't that the people loved him and honored him; it was that *his Father* did, a gift infinitely more valuable than the applause of those around him.

Above all, in winning God's favor, Jesus won life. That, after all, was the great promise to Adam and Eve right from the very beginning. If they violated God's law, threw off his authority and crown, and ate the fruit, they would die. But if they loved and obeyed him, fulfilling their God-given role as king and queen of the world under him, they would live. Jesus the Well-Pleasing One did just that—he loved and obeyed God as Adam and Eve had not—and therefore death's grip on humanity slipped in his presence. So he said to the girl who had died, "Little girl, . . . arise," and she did (Mark 5:41). He cried out to the dead Lazarus, "Lazarus, come out!" and the dead man came out (John 11:43). Instead of others' sickness infecting him when he touched and embraced them, his life infected them and drove out the uncleanness. Time and time again, when sickness and death thought their reign was unquestioned and absolute, Jesus rolled it back with the power of life. Here's how John put it: "As the Father has life in himself, so he has granted the Son also to have life in himself" (John 5:26). Jesus won the favor of God, and therefore he had—and *was*—life.

But then he died.

What a strange turn in the story! If Jesus really did earn God's favor and all its eternal rewards—the kingdom, joy, glory, even life—then the last thing you'd expect would be for him to die. No, what you'd expect is something more like what happened to Enoch ("He was not, for God took him" [Gen. 5:24]) or Elijah with his chariot of fire to heaven.

But none of that happened to Jesus. Jesus died, and in one of the most horrific ways human beings have ever invented. Why? Well, here's the answer: in everything Jesus did, from his life to his death to his resurrection, he wasn't acting just for himself. He was acting for and in the place of others.

Jesus the Champion

Now make no mistake here: Jesus most certainly *could have* acted just for himself. He could have lived a perfect life, met God's standards, earned God's favor and rewards, and ascended into heaven to the thunderous applause of a trillion angels. And that would have been that. But, of course, that wouldn't have done anything for *us* at all. If that had happened, Jesus's glory and honor as the Well-Pleasing One would have been his alone, and we would still be left in the lurch, rebels against God who have fallen woefully short of his glory. Jesus would have been honored, but we'd still be as desperate and as hopeless as ever.

But the fact that Jesus died, the fact that the One who actually earned life submitted to death, tells us that something more was happening. And that something more is the whole glory and joy of the Christian gospel. When Jesus won the favor of God and all its rewards, he wasn't doing it just for himself. He was doing it for others too. He was acting as a representative, a substitute, a champion. The idea of a representative is more or less familiar to us today. After all, we elect representatives to various levels of government, and we understand that those people will then go to state and national capitals and cast votes on our behalf. They represent us, they stand for us, and they speak for us. As common as it

71

is, though, I'm not sure that analogy ends up communicating very well about Jesus. After all, the last thing I want to leave people thinking is, "Jesus was a congressman?" There's not much glory in that. And there's certainly no love, no beating heart.

No, what we need is another way of understanding the role Jesus was filling. We need to understand a concept similar to but not identical with that of a representative. That's the role of the champion. To most of us, the word *champion* just means "the winner," that is, the person who won the tournament and gets the trophy. But that's not what the word originally meant.

A few years ago, during a vacation, my wife and I took our kids to a dinner theater called Medieval Times. Maybe you've heard of it. The restaurant is built to look like a medieval castle, with flags fluttering from the parapets, knights guarding the doors, and all the servers dressed in feudalistic garb. The real attraction, though, is that you eat dinner around a gigantic arena where knights literally joust with each other from horseback, fight with swords and maces, and compete in various other competitions. It's an incredible show. What keeps you really engaged as an audience member, though, is that at the very beginning of the experience you're assigned to one of four teams—red, yellow, blue, or green—and then with great fanfare you're introduced to your champion for the evening. For me and my family, this was the Blue Knight. If the Blue Knight won the entire tournament, the blue team would win a gift certificate to the gift shop.

For the rest of the evening, then, the Blue Knight *represented* me and my family. He jousted for us and raced for us and drew his sword and fought for us. And let me tell you, this was no congressman-like representation. My heart was 100 percent in this thing. This guy was my hero, and those were *my* battles he was fighting as much as they were his. He was fighting for us, on our behalf, in order to win *for us* something we could not win for ourselves.

Sadly, the Blue Knight lost. (I think it's because the dude actually broke his finger in a sword fight. He was a stud.) Even so, you should have seen my children's faces when he strode out into the lobby to sign autographs after the show was over, bandaged finger and all. My kids might as well have been looking into the face of King Arthur. They were awestruck, smiling up at him with dewy eyes and dumb grins, sheepishly asking for autographs and taking pictures. To them, this guy wasn't just an actor in a show. He was *their guy*. He was the one who had fought on their behalf. He was their champion.

That's precisely the role Jesus was filling in his life, death, and resurrection—but on a cosmic scale. When he undertook the mission of becoming human, fulfilling God's law, and living a perfect life, he was not doing it just for his own sake. He was doing it on behalf of others, as their representative and substitute and champion.

All this is part of why the Bible makes such a big deal about Jesus being king. Today kings are mostly figureheads; they wear extravagant clothes, make speeches, open parliament meetings, and greet other figureheads. In the ancient world, though, kings were far more than that. They were warriors, and their primary role was to serve as no less than their people's champion—fighting their battles, protecting them, and defending them against others. Do you remember the story of David and Goliath? One of the points of that story was to show that because David fought on behalf of Israel while Saul cowered, he—and not Saul—was the one God had chosen to be king. That's the kind of image that would have come to mind when the early Christians declared Jesus to be King. Kings fight; it's what they do. And therefore Jesus would fight for his people, representing them in battles they could not fight for themselves.

This idea of kingship and representation is a rich and fascinating part of the Bible's epic story. In fact, the Bible presents the entire history of humanity as a story of two great champion-kings. The first of those, of course, was the one we might call King Adam the Fallen, who stood as humanity's first champion and tragically dragged the entire world into insurrection against God. Paul puts it like this in Romans 5: "Sin came into the world through one man, and death through sin. . . . Because of one man's trespass, death reigned through that one man" (vv. 12, 17). It's really pretty clear: in his declaration of war against God, King Adam the Fallen represented us all and condemned us all to death.

Adam Was Our Best Shot

I have to be honest here. When I think about that story and its implications for my own life, my heart recoils against the whole idea. I mean, I never voted to elect Adam my representative; I didn't ask him to act for me in rebelling against God. So how can it be fair that *I* suffer consequences for something *he* did? Well, I don't want to pretend that's an easy question. It's not, and I'm not sure there's a slam-dunk, Tweet-worthy thing I can say that will pull all the tension out of it. In fact, I think God very well could have set up the world to function like we think we'd have wanted it—with each of us acting for ourselves, rising or falling on the goodness or badness of our own actions. And that would have been perfectly just and . . . fine. But on the other hand, I wonder if in thinking that way we're actually not giving God quite enough credit. Think about this: is it possible that in making Adam our champion-king, rather than letting (or making) us each stand on our own, God was actually letting us off easy? Is it possible that appointing Adam to represent us actually showed God's goodness and love better than having each of us go it alone?

I actually think that's the case. Think about it: of all the ten billion humans who have ever lived (except for Jesus, of course), Adam had the very best shot of actually doing what was necessary to win God's favor. After all, he was in a perfect environment with no external stress or distraction, he knew God face-to-face, and he was created as a grown man—which means he didn't have to live through the naïveté and immaturity of childhood, not to mention adolescence. He had every advantage in the world, and if he'd remained faithful to God, he would have won God's favor and its rewards. Once we understand all that, we can see how it was actually marvelously kind of God to tie all our fates to Adam. He was by far our best shot, uniquely privileged, and way more likely to succeed than any of us standing on our own.

Think of it like this: imagine you're attending a basketball game, and at halftime you're called down on the court for a three-point-shot challenge. The deal is pretty simple. You get one shot from the top of the key. If you make it, you win $10 billion, and you're set for life. But if you miss it, you don't just lose the money; you also have to go to a supermax prison for the rest of your life. There's no way out of it. You can't decline to participate, and there's no compromise; it's $10 billion or life in prison. Now I don't know about you, but I'd be panicked in that situation. Maybe you have more confidence in your shooting skills than I do, but the prospect of a life in the slammer would be staring me pretty hard in the face at this point. But imagine that the announcer then booms over the loudspeaker one more time: "But you have one more choice to make. You can take the shot yourself, or . . . you can let Steph Curry take it for you."

Now let me tell you, if Steph Curry strode out of the locker room at that moment, I'd look at him with dewier eyes than my daughter looked at the Blue Knight. I'd probably hug him, and then there would be not a question in the world: I'd hand Steph Curry the ball.

It's obviously not a perfect analogy, but I think that's pretty close to what was happening when God let Adam "take the shot for us" in the Garden of Eden. The stakes were enormous—life or death—and the reality is that the only chance any of us really had at winning was for someone else to do it for us. Yes, Adam "missed." (Actually, as we discussed earlier with the illustration from archery, he didn't just miss; he rebelled.) But even so, it's actually wonderful for us that God was establishing the principle that someone else could stand for us and act as our champion. It meant that, in time, he would send another champion to do what Adam failed to do—to make the shot and win salvation for us. That's what Jesus did as the second great champion-king of humanity. King Jesus the Favored picked up the sword that King Adam the Fallen dropped. He did as our champion what

Adam failed to do. He made the shot, lived the perfect life, and won God's favor.

Winning God's Favor Wasn't Enough; Jesus Had to Die

But there's one more thing: if Jesus was going to save his people, he couldn't just do what Adam failed to do. Why not? Because the curse Adam earned for his rebellion against God was still there. God's sentence against him, "You shall surely die" (Gen. 2:17), still hung over humanity's head like a sword. That's why Jesus couldn't simply ascend in glory to heaven. That's why he had to die. If he was truly going to save his people, he would have to save them in two ways—first by earning God's favor for them and then by exhausting the curse they deserved for their own failure. That's what Jesus was doing when he died on the cross. His death wasn't just an accident of history, or an example of love, or an illustration of how much our sin hurt God. It was King Jesus the Favored fulfilling his kingly role by allowing the curse to be executed on him—instead of on the people he was acting to save.

All this is why God so completely infused Jesus's crucifixion with kingly symbols and images, even in all their tragic irony. As he was scourged by the Roman soldiers, Jesus was dressed in a royal robe and given a scepter to hold . . . as mockery. As he was nailed to the cross, he was coronated . . . with a crown of thorns. As he struggled to breathe and finally died, a sign above his head proclaimed him to be "the King of the Jews." And yet with every one of those symbols, each designed to humiliate and degrade him, the mockers proclaimed more truth than they realized. I love the way one old pastor described this mind-blowing mystery:

When Christ uttered in the judgment hall of Pilate the remarkable words, "I am a king," he pronounced a sentiment fraught with unspeakable dignity and power. His enemies might deride his pretensions and express their mockery of his claim by presenting him with a crown of thorns, a reed, and a purple robe, and nailing him to the cross; but in the eyes of unfallen intelligences, he was a king. A higher power presided over that derisive ceremony, and converted it into a real coronation. That crown of thorns was indeed the diadem of empire; that purple robe was the badge of royalty; that fragile reed was the symbol of unbounded power; and that cross the throne of dominion which shall never end.[3]

As he died on the cross, King Jesus was finishing, once and for all, everything necessary to secure the salvation of his people. "It is finished!" he cried just before he died, and, of course, he was right. He had accomplished everything. Not only had he done everything necessary by his perfect life to win God's favor for his people, but now he was also exhausting in his own body the curse, death, and condemnation Adam had brought on them. The sword that hung over his people's heads found its sheath in *his* heart, not theirs.

Stop Playing in the Mud

Before we press on, let's stop and think about what all this means. By now I hope it's been drilled deeply into your heart that the concept of the favor of God isn't some low-stakes game of trying to convince God to pay our bills or buy us a nicer car or give us the cattle on a thousand hills. It's infinitely more important and profound than that. Nor is it a sort of niche doctrine that can be safely ignored and left to the confines of late-night Christian television. No, once you understand it correctly, the favor of God turns out to be right at the heart of the Christian gospel and intimately connected to the mission and work of Jesus Christ. The favor of God—his pleasure, his delight, his verdict of righteousness— is what each of us needs more than we need anything else in the world. It is what we exist for, what will bring us the most joy, what will secure eternity for us, and what will make us fully and truly human in the way God intended from the very beginning. And because we forfeited all that by our sin and rebellion against our Creator, the favor of God is *precisely* what Jesus Christ came to secure for us. It's what he won for us by his life lived in our place, his death died in our place, and his resurrection to new and eternal life.

Do you remember the quote from C. S. Lewis in the introduction to this book, that we can so easily be like a little boy who prefers making mud pies in the street because he has no idea what is meant by a vacation at the beach? When it comes to the favor of God, so many Christians are just like that little boy. We think God's favor is a matter of a little more money or slightly better circumstances in our lives, and then we concoct a backbreaking system whereby we have to scratch and scrape to convince God to give us the crumbs off his table. What a pile of mud that is! When God offers us his favor, it's not a matter of material blessings; it's the whole glittering treasure of eternal friendship with him and life everlasting. Dear Christian, stop playing in the mud! Stop thinking God's favor is found in your checkbook and attainable by something you can do. Lift up your eyes! When you do, you'll see that God's favor is infinitely more than you ever imagined, and it's been right there—always—in the hands of Jesus from the very beginning.

Yet there's still more to see and savor: Jesus's representation of his people isn't at all like a faceless politician casting a vote in a distant capital city. It's an intimate, heartfelt, covenantal union between him and his people that outstrips and transcends every other relationship imaginable. You see, we are not simply related to our King in some cold, formal, constitutional way. We are *united* to him in blood and love and life.

5

United to Christ, Favored by God

One of my favorite parts of my role as a pastor is when I'm invited to officiate a wedding. I realize that may strike you as a strange thing to say; most guys aren't exactly thrilled at the prospect of spending the better part of a Saturday dressed up and attending a ceremony and several hours of a reception. Personally, I could take or leave the reception, but I really do enjoy officiating the ceremony. Part of the fun is that you literally never know what's going to happen—except that there's just about a 100 percent certainty that one thing or another is going to go wrong. Maybe it'll be a bridesmaid who locks her knees and swoons in the middle of the service; or the little flower girl who sees someone she knows, stops to say hello, and refuses to go any farther; or the ring bearer who comes down the aisle at a full sprint!

I've had several of those experiences throughout my years of officiating weddings. There was the groom who was so nervous that he kept his eyes locked on me while saying his vows. "Say it to her," I said. "You're not marrying me." There was also the best man who lost the ring and the pianist who played the wrong song. And then there was the time *I* began the wedding before the mothers had been seated or the bride had made her way down the aisle. D'oh!

Those are the kinds of little mishaps that make weddings interesting, but what I really love about them is the moment when I—of all the people in the world—get to say *the* words that literally transform two people into something new. "Those whom God has joined together, let no man separate," I say. "Forasmuch as these two have consented together in holy marriage, and have witnessed the same before God and this congregation, I pronounce that they are . . . husband and wife."

Sometimes when the two people are close friends of mine, I've even been known to tease them a little, balking a time or two before I say those last three magic words. But the wonder of the whole thing is that once I say them—regardless of what went wrong beforehand or what struggles the couple had to endure to get there—a new and beautiful and intimate relationship is created. These two people, who a moment earlier were two separate individuals, are suddenly and really *united* in marriage. They become something different, something more, than they were just a moment before.

It's a sad truth that the spiritual reality of marriage has been all but lost in our day. Most people look at it as, at best, an antiquated tradition that now is mostly used for social engineering. It's a contract for the mutual benefit of two individuals; as long as the relationship is good for you, you stick with it, but once it's no longer of benefit, you execute the exit provision of the contract and move on. That's about all the world thinks of marriage these days. The Bible teaches, though, that marriage is far more than a contract. At the very least, it is a covenant made between two people—a set of promises that the bride and the groom make to each other before the watching world. That's why we call them wedding *vows*, after all; they're promises the bride and the groom make to each other before the listening, witnessing ears of the congregation.

But you know, there's even more to the reality of marriage than a covenant reveals. When two people are married, a spiritual union is created between them. They become, as the Bible says, "one flesh." Of course, that doesn't mean the bride and the groom cease to exist as individuals. I am still me, and my wife is still herself; that didn't change when we got married. But we are also something more now than just individuals who happen to live in the same house. God has united us in an intimate, real, covenantal, and spiritual relationship, and the passing years are only causing us to grow together more tightly and inextricably. What we share is not a contract. It's not a business relationship or a mere friendship. It's a real and vital and spiritual *union* with each other.

More Than Lord, King, or Friend

Did you know that the Bible actually uses marriage as a way of illustrating and explaining a believer's relationship with Jesus Christ? Perhaps the most famous passage where this happens is in Ephesians 5, where Paul spends two paragraphs talking about the relationship between a husband and a wife and then at the end turns and says, "This mystery is profound, and I am saying that it refers to Christ and his church" (v. 32). What a surprising turn! The relationship of marriage, he is saying, actually parallels and helps us to understand the relationship between Jesus and a believer. I wonder if you've ever thought of your relationship with Jesus in that way. Sometimes the language we use to describe Jesus can make him seem so distant and formal. Oh sure, we talk about having a "personal relationship" with him, but then we major on words such as *Lord*, *King*, or perhaps at best *Friend*. That's not to say these words are wrong. They're actually profoundly right. But the truth is we don't normally think of the relationship we might have with a Lord, King, or even Friend being marked by the same intimacy and tenderness and closeness that characterize a relationship with a spouse. Marriage is a special and unique union, and Paul says *that's* what most closely approximates the character of our relationship with Jesus.

But notice this too: as intimate and rich as a marriage relationship is, even it can't fully encompass the richness of our relationship with Jesus. How do we know that? Because marriage is just one of several images and metaphors the Bible uses to describe our relationship with him. We are said to be his brothers, his children, bricks in a building built on him as the foundation, parts of a body with him as the head, even branches connected to him as the life-giving vine. No one of these images alone embraces the full reality of how we are related to Christ, but when we take them together, the picture they paint is mind-blowing and life-changing. As a believer, you are intimately and vitally *united* to Jesus

Christ. You are in him, and he is in you, and the ramifications of that truth are explosive.

Union with Christ

Don't let those last couple of sentences rush by you too quickly. This is profound and powerful stuff. In fact, I would argue that this idea of our union with Christ is, dollar for dollar, the most underappreciated, underemphasized, and overlooked doctrine in all of Christian theology. And yet it is the very foundation and root of the gospel. This reality—that we as believers are not just in *contract* with Jesus but really, truly, vitally, spiritually, and intimately *united* to him—is precisely what secures our salvation from sin and makes it right and good and fitting. This reality is what makes it just and righteous for God to pour out on us—sinners and rebels—his favor. Let's take a deeper look at all this together.

One of the most fascinating places in the Bible that refer to our union with Christ is in Romans 6. Take a look:

> What shall we say then? Are we to continue in sin that grace may abound? By no means! How can we who died to sin still live in it? Do you not know that all of us who have been baptized into Christ Jesus were baptized into his death? We were buried therefore with him by baptism into death, in order that, just as Christ was raised from the dead by the glory of the Father, we too might walk in newness of life. (vv. 1–4)

At first glance, it looks as if Paul is just raising an obvious objection to what he's been teaching so far in his letter—that we can never be saved by *earning* God's favor but that Jesus wins God's favor *for us*. The objection he raises is one that's been made a thousand times against Christianity, and it goes like this: "If we are saved by grace and not by earning God's favor through our works, then we can live however we want, right? We can go on sinning as much as we want, can't we?" Not surprisingly, Paul gives a really straightforward answer to that question: "No, you can't do that." In fact, you can read these verses as if Paul is a frustrated old man batting away an irritating question. "By no means! . . . Don't you know?" It sounds downright mean.

But I don't think that is what is happening. Paul isn't frustrated with the question. In fact, throughout these verses, he is *using* the question to uncover this explosive truth about our relationship with Jesus. And he's doing it a little at a time, with a grin and a sparkle in his eyes, like an excited father at Christmas bringing out one present after another to the delight of his children. Do you see it? First, he raises this fairly obvious objection: "Then we can just go on sinning, can't we?" Then he gives the blindingly obvious answer: "No, you can't." But then look at what he does at the end of verse 2: "How can we who *died to sin* still live in it?"

Yes, yes, of course, Paul. Got it. Clearly, I can't go on sinning because I died to sin . . . whoa, whoa, whoa, hold up a second there, Paul. What did you just say? What's this about Christians having *died to sin*? When exactly did *that* happen, and what on earth does it mean?

If that's how you reacted when you read that verse, then it worked exactly as Paul intended. He meant it to shock and surprise. See, this idea that we died to sin is a completely new idea in Romans, and it comes flying in right out of the blue. Paul hasn't said anything remotely like it in the entire book, and yet here he just tosses it out on the table. As a Christian, you have already died to sin. We're supposed to hear that idea, do a double take, and think, "What an incredible thing to say. What do you mean, Paul? How have we died? When did we die? Is that just a metaphor or a rhetorical flourish? Is it just an illustration that maybe went a little too far? What do you mean we have died?"

Over the next few verses, Paul pulls back the veil a little more. So in verses 3–4, he makes it clear when this dying to sin happened. It was when we were baptized—in other words, when we became believers in Jesus and declared to the world that we are with him. (Just by the way, Paul isn't making an argument here that baptism is necessary for salvation or that it actually in any way does the saving. He's just pointing to it as the beginning point—the starting gun, so to speak—for the Christian life. When you're baptized as a believer, you're saying publicly to heaven and to hell and to all the world, "This is where I plant my flag. I am with King Jesus now!") Anyway, Paul says *that's* when it happened, *that's* when you died to sin—when you became a Christian. And look how he defines the nature of that dying at the end of verse 3. What he means by saying "you died" is that you were baptized "into his death." In verse 4, he gets even more specific. When you were baptized, you were "buried . . . with him by baptism into death."

Now pause and think about this for a second, because it's a deep and profound truth. When you became a Christian and entered into a relationship with Jesus, when you proclaimed to the world by baptism that you are now with him, God created a union between you and Jesus so close, so intimate, and so vital that what happened to him can also be said to have happened to you. He died, *and you died*. He was raised from the dead, *and you were raised to newness of life* (and will be raised from the dead on the last day). Here's how Paul joyously describes this truth in verse 5, finally holding the entire thing up like an artist unveiling his finished work: "If we have been united with him in a death like his, we shall certainly be united with him in a resurrection like his."

The crucial word in that verse is *united*, and it literally means "grown together." Originally, it's a word from horticulture, and it refers to what happens when you graft a branch onto a vine. In time, that branch "grows together" with the vine until it is united in every way with its new plant. That's what your relationship with Jesus is like, Paul says. You are united to him like a branch to a vine, such that there is a vital, intimate, and living union between you and him.

Saul, Why Are You Persecuting Me?

If you think about it, *united* is the perfect word to describe this relationship, because it captures exactly what Jesus meant when he told his disciples, "I am the vine; you are the branches" (John 15:5). Paul didn't come up with this idea that we are united to Christ by himself; he learned it from Jesus. In fact, this truth and its implications would have been pressed deeply into Paul's heart by his experience on the road to Damascus. The story is told in Acts 9. At the time, Paul had a different name—Saul—and he was a very different person than the apostle who wrote half of the New Testament. In the story told in Acts 9, he was actually on his way to the city of Damascus to persecute Christians, probably by confiscating their property, throwing them in prison, or perhaps even killing them. As he was on the way, though, something extraordinary happened, and it shattered Saul's world:

> Suddenly a light from heaven shone around him. And falling to the ground, he heard a voice saying to him, "Saul, Saul, why are you persecuting me?" And he said, "Who are you, Lord?" And he said, "I am Jesus, whom you are persecuting. But rise and enter the city, and you will be told what you are to do." The men who were traveling with him stood speechless, hearing the voice but seeing no one. Saul rose from the ground, and although his eyes were opened, he saw nothing. So they led him by the hand and brought him into Damascus. (vv. 3–8)

To make a long story short, Paul eventually met a Christian who told him the good news about Jesus, and Paul became a Christian. But what I want you to see in these verses is exactly what Jesus said to Paul (then Saul) when he confronted him on the road. Do you see it there in verses 4–5? Jesus asked him, "Saul, Saul, why are you persecuting *me*?" And then when Saul asked, "Who are you, Lord?" Jesus answered, "I am Jesus, *whom you are persecuting.*"

Now wait a second. Why did Jesus say that Saul was persecuting *him*? After all, Saul wasn't persecuting *Jesus*, not personally. Jesus was enthroned in heaven, and there was no way Saul could get there to cause him trouble. He was persecuting *Christians*, not Jesus. Right? And yet Jesus said twice that by persecuting his people, Saul was persecuting him. Do you see the significance of that? The risen Lord Jesus Christ so completely identifies with his people that when Saul was persecuting *them*, he was actually persecuting Jesus himself. In a profound and vital way that Paul was only beginning to understand, Jesus is *united* to his people.

Christ Is in Us, and We Are in Christ

But still, what does all this actually mean, and what are the implications of it? What difference does it make in our lives? The Bible talks about our union with Christ hundreds of times, but many of those verses use two phrases that we tend to read over without really noticing. In fact, many times we probably just chalk up these two phrases to a little "Christianese" and barely give them a second thought. And yet they are absolutely chock-full of meaning. These two phrases are "Christ is in us" and "we are in Christ." Once you realize that these two ideas are talking about your union with Christ, you'll see that reality on almost every page of the Bible, and you'll have discovered a treasury with riches enough to last you a lifetime. Let's take a look at them.

The idea that Christ is in us shows up dozens of times in the New Testament. Paul asks in 2 Corinthians 13:5, "Do you not realize this about yourselves, that Jesus Christ is in you?" In Romans 8:10, he says straightforwardly, "Christ is in you," and in Ephesians 3:17, he says that Jesus "dwells in your hearts through faith." In Colossians 1:27, he says that the great mystery of the gospel itself is "Christ in you, the hope of glory," and in Galatians 2:20, he goes so far as to say, "It is no longer I who live, but Christ who lives in me."

All this, of course, comes from what Jesus said in John 15 about the vine and the branches:

Abide in me, and I in you. As the branch cannot bear fruit by itself, unless it abides in the vine, neither can you, unless you abide in me. I am the vine; you are the branches. Whoever abides in me and I in him, he it is that bears much fruit, for apart from me you can do nothing. (vv. 4–5)

This image is so beneficial in helping us understand what it means that Christ is in us. Here's why. In a grapevine like the one Jesus was talking about, the life and energy of the vine itself enliven and empower each branch. Sap and fluid flow from the root and the vine through the entire plant, and the result is life and fruit in the branches. Put simply, the life of the vine is *in* the branches, and the life of the branches is utterly dependent on the vine. Jesus was saying that the same thing is true of him and you if you're a believer. You are united to him like a branch to a vine, and his resurrection life and power pulse and flow through you. I hope you can see the ramifications of all this, because they're enormous.

For one thing, understanding that your spiritual life is not inherent to you but flows to you from the Vine is deeply humbling. You are spiritually alive because—and only because—you are united to the Source of all life, and if you were to be separated from him, you would die. It's as Jesus said in the next verse: "If anyone does not abide in me he is thrown away like a branch and withers" (John 15:6). You live because Jesus lives.

Not only that, but this reality that Christ is in us is also radically transforming. I'm no horticulturist, but those I know tell me that you can actually graft a fruitless grape or olive branch onto a strong, healthy plant and in time that branch will begin to grow and produce fruit! The life and sap of the healthy plant push into the fruitless branch and literally transform it, making it something new and beautiful. In the same way, when we put our faith in Jesus and are united to him, his resurrection life begins to pulse through us, transforming our hearts, our minds, our experiences, and even our suffering into something beautiful and alive. The dead places in our lives begin to bloom! That's the power of Christ in us.

The Bible says something else about our union with Jesus. Not only is Christ in us, but we as believers are also in Christ. This idea, too, shows up dozens of times throughout the New Testament. Have you ever noticed how many times the Bible uses the phrase "in Christ" or "in the Lord"? This is the truth those phrases point to. Just as Christ is in us, we are also in him. We often tend to read over these words without thinking, but they're more than just a bit of religious jargon. They point to a deep and profound and powerful truth—one that has its roots in the eternal heart and purpose of God. After all, the Bible says it was part of God's plan all the way back in eternity past that we would be united to his Son. So in Ephesians, Paul says, "[God] chose us in him before the foundation of the world" (1:4). And in 2 Timothy, he says, "[God] saved us . . . not because of our works but because of his own purpose and grace, which he gave us in Christ Jesus before the ages began" (1:9). Do you see? If you're a Christian, then God has been planning his salvation of you for ages upon ages. You are not an afterthought to him. You didn't just "squeak in" at the last second. No, all the way back in eternity past, God gave you to Jesus, placed you in him, and united you to him.

The most important truth to realize here is that if you are in Christ, then his life, death, and resurrection are also counted as yours. In other words, what happened to Jesus, God reckons as having happened to you too by virtue of your union with him. That's why Paul can say something so astonishing as "You died to sin." That's obviously not saying the nails actually went through your hands, but it's also not just a metaphor or an illustration. Paul is actually unveiling a spiritual truth that's infinitely deeper. Because you are united to Christ—because you are "in him"—God conceived of you as doing in and with Christ *the very same things he did*. In other words, what Jesus did, God says you did. The implications of this are stunning. When Jesus lived a perfect life, God thought of it as *you* living a perfect life. When Jesus died, God thought of it as *you* dying. When Jesus rose from the dead, that same resurrection power ignited spiritual life in *you*. And when history comes to an end, that same life and power will resurrect *your body* from the grave. Jesus's life is and will be your life; his triumph is and will be your triumph. Even now, the Bible says, God has "raised us up with him and seated us with him in the heavenly places in Christ Jesus" (Eph. 2:6). Somehow, in a profoundly mysterious and yet very real way, Jesus sits enthroned in heaven . . . and therefore so do we. Because we are united to him.

Your Salvation Is Therefore Right and Good and Just and Fitting

All this is one of the most profound spiritual truths in the universe, and it lies like a diamond at the heart of the gospel of Jesus Christ. It actually explains why it is *right* and *just* and *good* and *fitting* that God should save us. We are—vitally, really, spiritually—united to Jesus like branches to a vine and like members to a body. And the upshot of this is that what is yours becomes his, and what is his becomes yours. On the one hand, this means that because you are united to Jesus, God credited your sin to him. He looked on Jesus his Son as if all your sin was *his*, and he sacrificed him because of it. The curse was executed on Jesus, not on you. The sword of God's wrath sank into *his* heart, not yours. And you were free.

On the other hand, though, God also credited his perfect life to you. Do you understand what that means? The glorious truth is that if you are a Christian, you don't simply stand before God with a clean slate or a second chance. You actually have the overflowing favor and pleasure of God. The King of heaven looks down on you from his throne, smiling and singing and exulting over you, and he says, "With this one I am well pleased!" But he doesn't do that because *you* did anything to earn or win his favor. No, Jesus has God's favor by right. He won it; he earned it. And because you are united to Jesus, God *credits* his life to you and gives you his favor.

It's really a terrible misunderstanding of Christianity to think God is simply giving us a second chance or a clean slate. If that were the case, we'd be in no better shape than before, because we'd all mess up our clean slate almost immediately. But thank God the gospel is really much better news than that! God doesn't give us just a clean slate. He gives us *Jesus's slate*. His record of perfect obedience is credited to us, and we live because of it. And at the same time, our slate—our record of sin and rebellion against God—is credited to him, and he dies because of it. What a magnificent exchange!

Jesus receives our sin, and we receive his righteousness.

He suffers, and we rejoice.

He is mocked, and we are honored.

He is rejected, and we are welcomed.

He dies, and we live!

And that's only the beginning. All the blessings and rewards of God's favor pour down on Jesus's head like oil. Kingdom and life and sonship and righteousness and honor and glory—they're all his by right. He earned them. And yet because we are united to him, they flow down on us as well.

Do you realize that God doesn't give the blessings of eternity directly to you? He gives them to Jesus because Jesus earned them. They're his by right. You get them only because you're united to him. So Jesus is declared righteous, and therefore you are declared righteous. Jesus has life in himself, and so you have been given spiritual life. Jesus was resurrected, and so you will be resurrected. Jesus is glorified, and so you will be glorified. All those rewards and blessings are his—and therefore they are yours too. Thank God that what happens to the Vine also happens to us, the branches.

Rest in Jesus

Well, congratulations! There was some deep biblical and theological diving in these last two chapters. But you know, sometimes it's good to trade in the snorkel for some scuba gear and really plumb the depths of the Bible's wonders. I think that's true when it comes to the favor of God. There is so much more beauty and wonder and color and life—and gospel—in that reality than we usually give it credit for.

I wonder if your conception of the favor of God has changed as we've explored its deeper meaning in the Bible.

Have you realized that God's favor is not some cherry on top of the Christian life that only the really good Christians get? I hope so. I also hope you've discovered that the favor of God is not something you'll ever be able to win for yourself, that your only hope of getting it—of being well pleasing to God—is to be united to the One of whom God said, "This is my beloved Son, with whom I am well pleased." Rest in Jesus, dear Christian. Your salvation is secure in his strong hand. God is pleased with you, and he will cease to be pleased with you only when he ceases to be pleased with his own Son. You will lose God's favor only when Jesus loses God's favor. And that will never happen.

As I was beginning to write this book, I told one of my friends that I was writing about the biblical idea of the favor of God. "Wow," he said. "That's kind of a niche topic." I smiled and didn't press the matter, but I hope you can see now that my friend was wrong. God's favor isn't a niche topic at all. We let it become niche because for whatever set of reasons we more or less surrendered the idea to health-and-wealth preachers who used it as both a stick and a carrot to get people to send money to their "ministries." But the favor of God isn't a niche topic, and we would do well to re-assert its true place and meaning at the heart of the Christian gospel. After all, to be justified—to be declared righteous and pleasing to God—is to receive God's favor. It is to have God turn his face toward us in acceptance and delight. And that happens not by works, not by deserving or earning or winning it, but only by being united through faith to Jesus the Well-Pleasing One, the Favored One.

What's more, the blessings and gifts that pour down from heaven to us because God's favor rests on us are infinitely more valuable than any prosperity teacher would have us believe. God's favor is not so cheap that its best gifts can be spent, wasted, and wrecked in an afternoon. When God pours out the blessings of his favor, they are the kind that have infinite value now and that last into eternity.

It's time to see what Jesus our Champion has won for us!

PART 2

THE BLESSINGS OF GOD'S FAVOR

6

The Blessing of Contentment

In 1893, the very first members of my church, Third Avenue Baptist in Louisville, made a covenant with one another—a set of promises that formalized their union together as a local church and defined how they intended to live together as brothers and sisters in Christ. Among other things, they promised with God's help to "walk together in brotherly love," to "exercise a Christian care and watchfulness over each other," and to "endeavor by example and effort to win souls to Christ." As far as we can tell, that covenant has never been changed. For over 120 years, every member of Third Avenue Baptist Church has made those promises.

One of the most beautiful and gritty promises we make to one another is this: "We covenant with one another that, God enabling us, we will participate in each other's joys, and endeavor with tenderness and sympathy to bear each other's burdens and sorrows." Based on Paul's encouragements to the church in Romans 12:15 and Galatians 6:2, that portion of our covenant captures the heartbeat of our church more than any other. We love one another, and we try to show that love in tangible, immediately obvious ways—whether it's rejoicing with those who rejoice or weeping with those who weep.

Through the years, I've noticed that when people make that promise, they usually assume that participating in others' joys will wind up being easier than bearing others' burdens and sorrows. Sometimes that's true. When someone's child is in the hospital or when cancer is diagnosed, bearing that burden is far from easy. But it turns out that it's not always easy to participate in someone else's joy either. Especially when the joy you're supposed to celebrate is one you wanted for yourself but didn't receive. That's when it gets hard—that's when it requires grace—to rejoice with those who rejoice.

Soon after I came to Third Avenue as senior pastor, I was reminded in an unforgettably beautiful way just how true this reality is. The church was not very big, a hundred members or so, and there were two particular couples who had been asking the church to pray for them for the past two years. Both were struggling with infertility. Because of and through their struggle, these two couples had become fast and solid friends, supporting and encouraging one another and praying for one another through the sadness, disappointment, dashed hope, and heartsickness that always accompany prolonged infertility. They'd even joined the same home group so they would have a built-in way to see and care for one another regularly. They shared a precious friendship, and the entire church knew of it and treasured it.

Our church gathers together twice every Sunday, once for the main service in the morning and then again in the evening for prayer. At the evening service, we hear about happenings in the life of the church and also in individual members' lives. Engagements are announced, prayers are lifted up for unsaved neighbors and family members, and a hundred other joys and sorrows are shared and embraced by the church. At one of those services, maybe a year after I arrived as pastor, one of the couples stood up during the evening service and announced with tears and great joy that God had finally answered the church's prayers. She was pregnant! God had given them a baby!

I've never seen the church erupt in such joy as it did on that night. But the celebration was shorter lived than it might otherwise have been, because everyone in the room, having felt joy for the one couple, almost immediately felt heartbreak for the other. "What about them?" was the question on every mind, joy and heartbreak mingling in every heart.

My usual way of handling our prayer time is to ask someone seated nearby to pray for the person making the request. Before I could do that in this case, though, I saw a hand rising up and heard a voice softly but unmistakably saying, "I want to pray for them." It was the husband of the other couple, the best friend forged in the fire of a trial that God had now ended in his friend's life but not in his own. That dear Christian man stood and prayed—with tears in his eyes, with evident struggle, but also with real rejoicing—and he thanked God for giving to his friends a precious gift that he and his wife still desperately wanted for themselves.

I've often thought about that prayer and marveled at the grace that must have been flowing through that brother's life to enable him to pray it. He could have sat silently and said nothing that night, but he decided to lift up his voice in praise to the God who had *not* given him the gift of a child. He could have so desired and so treasured that particular gift from God's hand that the Lord's withholding of it could have caused him to doubt God's goodness altogether. He could have become embittered that God had decided to give that gift to someone else—to his friend, no less. But he did none of that. Instead, even in such heartbreaking circumstances, he saw a reason to praise God for his goodness.

This dear brother knew that the favor of God in his life was about far more than a particular earthly blessing—even one as desirable and good as a child. He understood that God's favor, won for him by Jesus Christ, has an eternal horizon. So he set his eyes on eternity and found the strength to walk through this life's laughter *and* tears with peaceful contentment.

Favor Brings Contentment

I think my friend's and his wife's contentment in those days is so extraordinary at least in part because—no matter how many good things happen in our lives, or how many of our wishes come true, or how many of our desires are fulfilled— the world around us is always pushing us to be discontent and anxious for more. It tells us to worry and be fearful, either about getting what we don't have or keeping what we do have. No one is immune to worry and discontent, and no one escapes anxiety.

It's wonderful therefore to know that Jesus himself addressed this very problem of anxiety and fear in his Sermon on the Mount. And what he said is that his intention for us—as his redeemed and now-favored children—is exactly the opposite. It's that our lives as Christians should be filled with a deep sense of peaceful contentment, not with anxiety and worry. Here's what Jesus says in Matthew 6:

> Therefore I tell you, do not be anxious about your life, what you will eat or what you will drink, nor about your body, what you will put on. . . . But seek first the kingdom of God and his righteousness, and all these things will be added to you. (vv. 25, 33)

We'll talk about the entire passage in more detail in a moment, but let's pause first to notice that there's a profound irony here when it comes to the way most people think about the concept of the favor of God. It's this: if you think God's favor is mostly about getting material gifts in this earthly age, then that misunderstanding will actually tend to stir up a cyclone of anxiety in your life. That's because you'll think those material blessings (however you've decided to define them) really are God's will for you, but you'll also convince yourself that the reason you don't have them is because you're doing something wrong—not having the right attitude, or not having enough faith, or not asking earnestly enough, or whatever. It's a double whammy: you don't get what you want, and God is disappointed in you to boot.

But once you understand that the favor of God is really about the friendship and delight of God, that you've forfeited those things entirely by your sin, and that only through faith in Jesus the Well-Pleasing One can you get them . . . well, then your life becomes stabilized by the ballast of eternity. Your eyes are set on heaven, you know beyond all doubt that God is working all things together for your good, and therefore you can live through the ups and downs of this life—the gifts granted *and* the gifts withheld—with a deep-running sense of peaceful contentment. In fact, contentment is one of the greatest blessings imaginable of living your life under God's favor in Jesus.

One Single-Hearted, Clear-Eyed Pursuit

Let's look more closely at what Jesus says in Matthew 6 about material blessings from God. Actually, the relevant portion begins a few verses earlier, where Jesus is telling his disciples what following him really means. Following him is not just a matter of outward conformity to a set of rules, he says, but a single-hearted, clear-eyed pursuit of love for and obedience to him that puts all other pursuits and passions in a distant backseat. So important is this point, in fact, that Jesus makes it three times over the course of six verses by using three images.

First, he tells his disciples that they should take care where they are stocking up their treasures:

> Do not lay up for yourselves treasures on earth, where moth and rust destroy and where thieves break in and steal, but lay up for yourselves treasures in heaven, where neither moth nor rust destroys and where thieves do not break in and steal. For where your treasure is, there your heart will be also. (Matt. 6:19–21)

Jesus's point is simple but profound: you can spend your life gathering up treasures for yourself here on earth, but you shouldn't, because they won't last. Rust corrodes cars, boats, and houses; moths destroy Italian suits and Louis Vuitton shoes; and thieves steal everything else. So don't plan to find contentment in such transient things. Instead, Jesus says, gather up for yourself treasures in heaven, treasures that will last forever. Why? The reason is not just because treasures you can't lose are better than treasures you can. The far more important reason is that your heart will long to be wherever your treasure is. Think about that, because it's critical for understanding how to think about the favor of God. If your most treasured possessions—if your most longed-for desires—are here on earth, then your love will be here as well, and you will not long as you should to be with Jesus. But if your most beloved possession is Jesus himself—if the favor of God is precious to you above all because it means you are his friend—then your heart will be with him, and you'll long to be in his presence. The heart of a Christian doesn't long to have *more here*; it longs to be with *him there*.

Jesus makes the same point in the next verses, this time with the image of a focused eye:

> The eye is the lamp of the body. So, if your eye is healthy, your whole body will be full of light, but if your eye is bad, your whole body will be full of darkness. If then the light in you is darkness, how great is the darkness! (Matt. 6:22–23)

Again, Jesus's point is that his followers should focus on the right things. The language can be a little obscure here, but he's playing on the idea that the eye guides the body and lets light into the body. So he's asking the question again, "Where are your eyes set? What are you looking toward and striving for?" If your eye is "healthy," Jesus says—if it's looking in the right direction and focused on what really matters—then your whole body (that is, your whole life) will be full of light and peace and contentment. But if not—if your eye is drawn away to lesser things, if it's set on wrong, unworthy, and temporary things—then your life will be full of darkness. You will be anxious and grasping and miserable.

The last image Jesus uses in these verses is of a servant pulled in two directions by two masters:

> No one can serve two masters, for either he will hate the one and love the other, or he will be devoted to the one and despise the other. You cannot serve God and money. (Matt. 6:24)

Jesus is making the same point here as in the previous two images. A person simply cannot serve two masters. You can't do part-time service to King Jesus and part-time service to another king. And if you try, Jesus says, you're going to wind up loving one of those masters and despising the other. One will inevitably become an unwelcome distraction, a cramp in the other's style. So Jesus asks here, "Whom will you serve? What will be your overarching, driving passion?" He puts the idea sharply in the last sentence: "You cannot serve God and money." The word used isn't really *money*, though. It's broader, something more like *stuff*. The point is crystal clear: you can't spend your life pining after material things and be the kind of eternity-minded person that one who is *truly* favored by God will be.

Jesus's call to his people here is bracing: if you are truly united to Jesus and therefore enjoying the favor of God, then your treasure will be in heaven, not here on earth. Your eyes will be focused on eternity, not on this life. And you will burn up your life in service to God, not in pursuit of the material gifts God sometimes gives. That's what will mark one who is truly united to Jesus, who is truly a Christian, who is truly favored by God. That kind of person will, as Jesus says in Matthew 6:33, "seek first the kingdom of God."

When Anxiety Attacks

Okay, so Jesus wants us to be single-mindedly focused on pursuing him and his kingdom. That's great, but let's be honest. I wish my life could look like that! I wish every hour of my day was a glassy sea of contentment set aflame with a passionate, joyful pursuit of Jesus. But, sadly, it's not. And I'll hazard a guess that yours isn't either. Why isn't it? Well, I think it's because of what Jesus talks about in the next few verses of the Sermon on the Mount. It's because I get anxious. I get worried and discontent about the things of this world. I'm like Peter walking on the water. I'm doing fine until I see the waves around me, lapping at my ankles and eventually my knees, and then I start to worry about what's going to happen to me . . . or what's *not* going to happen . . . or what's *already* happened . . . or what *hasn't* happened. My worry always attacks from every direction at once. And that's when I take my eyes off Jesus and start thinking about how I'm going to keep myself from sinking.

But, of course, you know what happens then. My heart begins to grasp for those earthly treasures and possessions about which I'm anxious, my eyes focus myopically on them, and before long I'm slaving away under the whip of King

Money or King Influence or King Success or King Reputation instead of joyously and peacefully serving King Jesus.

Anxiety, worry, and discontent are not a problem for just some of us. They are a problem for all of us. Oh, I try not to let on too much, but I get anxious. I worry. I worry about my kids, I worry about money, I worry about my reputation, and I worry about my church. I worry about all kinds of things that disturb my peace and stir up discontent in my heart. Maybe you're like me in that. Or maybe your struggle with worry and discontent is a thousand times worse. Maybe for you discontent and anxiety are so intense that you live your life in a perpetual state of suffocating worry, and no matter how much you'd like to pursue Jesus with joy and peace and contentment, that goal seems like it's a million miles away. If that's you, though, I hope you will take heart in knowing that Jesus knows you have that struggle—and he knew many of his followers through the centuries would share it. After all, that's why Jesus takes those anxieties head-on here in the Sermon on the Mount. Dear Christian, if you're bound up and miserable under the weight of a thousand anxieties, then these words of Jesus in Matthew 6:25–34 are specifically for you:

> Therefore I tell you, do not be anxious about your life, what you will eat or what you will drink, nor about your body, what you will put on. Is not life more than food, and the body more than clothing? Look at the birds of the air: they neither sow nor reap nor gather into barns, and yet your heavenly Father feeds them. Are you not of more value than they? And which of you by being anxious can add a single hour to his span of life? And why are you anxious about

clothing? Consider the lilies of the field, how they grow: they neither toil nor spin, yet I tell you, even Solomon in all his glory was not arrayed like one of these. But if God so clothes the grass of the field, which today is alive and tomorrow is thrown into the oven, will he not much more clothe you, O you of little faith? Therefore do not be anxious, saying, "What shall we eat?" or "What shall we drink?" or "What shall we wear?" For the Gentiles seek after all these things, and your heavenly Father knows that you need them all. But seek first the kingdom of God and his righteousness, and all these things will be added to you. Therefore do not be anxious about tomorrow, for tomorrow will be anxious for itself. Sufficient for the day is its own trouble.

Here's the amazing thing about what Jesus says here. This passage is full of the good news that Jesus doesn't intend for us to be filled with discontent and worry. He says so in fact three times in that one paragraph. "Do not be anxious. . . . Do not be anxious. . . . Therefore do not be anxious" (Matt. 6:25, 31, 34). It's wonderful, isn't it, that Jesus would care about something like that? It's wonderful that he didn't just say, "Follow me. And concerning that other stuff, just suck it up!" No, he wants our following of him to be a joyous, peacefully content following—not one we just slog through all the time. And so he gives us seven truths here that have incredible power to unlock the chains of worry in our lives. Let's take a look at them.

First, Jesus says that the best things in life don't have anything to do with material things. That's what he means by asking in verse 25, "Is not life more than food, and the body more than clothing?" In other words, what is it that food and clothing really get for us? What benefit do they bring? Yes, of course, they bring us some pleasure—I've eaten a mind-blowingly good steak or two in my life—and obviously they're part of what it takes to keep us alive. But think about both of those things a little more deeply. In fact, think about *every* material thing and the pleasure you might derive from having all of them without limit and without measure. Is that really all God's favor is good for—an all-you-can-eat buffet in a free-rent tuxedo at a really nice house? How ridiculous! And how insulting to the God of the universe to think so. No, friend, if you are a Christian, then you have promises from God that outstrip all those things. What God has in store for you in heaven, won for you by Jesus's work on your behalf, is *infinitely* better than any pleasure the things of this world could ever give. It's as David says in Psalm 16:11: "You make known to me the path of life; in your presence there is fullness of joy; at your right hand are pleasures forevermore."

Second, Jesus reminds us that God is able to provide material things for us—and it's no challenge for him at all. Look at the birds, Jesus says. They don't sow seed or reap crops or gather grain into their little bird barns. They don't give a single thought to whether or not their next meal is already in the pantry, and they certainly don't worry about whether that next meal is organic. And yet God feeds them. In all their oblivious ignorance, day after day as they work and hunt and peck and pull worms out of the ground, God takes care of them. He's effortlessly able to provide material things for his creatures, including us, and he proves it over and over every day by caring even for the birds of the air. That's a profoundly simple point, yes, but it's not one that is wasted on most of us. We need to hear this and be reminded of it over and over again. Our God is immensely powerful. He is able to provide us with all the material things we need—and even many things we don't really need but think we do. That in itself—remembering that providing for us is no challenge for our God—is sometimes enough to loosen our anxiety and to help us live in trust and peaceful contentment.

Third, Jesus tells us that worry doesn't do any good. It won't add a single hour to the length of our lives (Matt. 6:27). Worrying about something doesn't do anything at all to get that thing into our hands. Nor does worrying do a single thing to keep a fear from coming true. In fact, all worry does is make us miserable while we're living out the hours God has given us.

Fourth, Jesus says that God delights to provide for us. This is what he means when he talks about the grass of the field in verse 30. This point is similar to the point about the birds, but Jesus pushes it a step further. God doesn't just clothe the grasses of the field; he clothes them in *splendor*. He decks them out in colors and patterns that leave us dazzled with their beauty. You see? The point is not that God *can* provide for us but that he *delights* to do so. He is a joyful God whose goodness and generosity flow out of him like a flood—even to the grass we walk on. What an important reminder to us who are so prone to anxiety and discontent. We serve a God who is not only powerful but also joyfully, gladly, ecstatically good. And even more wonderfully, our God loves us, delights in us, favors us, and wants to do good for us.

I realize this is a difficult point in some ways, because there are times when we don't see God doing good to us. Maybe you're thinking that very thing now as you read these words: "I sure don't see God adorning me like a flower now. I don't see him overflowing with goodness and generosity toward me now." There are a few things to say in this regard that might be helpful.

For one thing, we need to remember that the flood of God's goodness and blessings does not come to us fully and finally until we stand in his presence in heaven. One day, dear friend, your shoulders—even if they're stooped in suffering now—are going to be clothed in royal robes. One day your head—even if it's bowed under hardship now—is going to be crowned in gold. So be patient and endure. One day God will call you home, and then it will be for you as Paul said:

> I have fought the good fight, I have finished the race, I have kept the faith. Henceforth there is laid up for me the crown of righteousness, which the Lord, the righteous judge, will award to me on that day, and not only to me but also to all who have loved his appearing. (2 Tim. 4:7–8)

Are you suffering now? Don't let it for a moment make you doubt God's goodness. Let it cause you to long even more for the day of his appearing.

Not only so, but remember too that God provides exactly what is sufficient for you to accomplish the work he has for you. He gives you what you need to do what he has planned for you, not what you might want him to give. The fact is, for many of us, our beef with God isn't that he's not providing for us; it's that he's not providing for us *in the way we want to be provided for*. Even as you ask for more, God might be saying to you, "My child, if I gave you those kingly robes now, you wouldn't be able to run the race I've set before you. If I gave you what you think you need, if I took that thorn out of your flesh now, you wouldn't be able to do what I've called you to do." Christian, trust in the Lord's goodness and wisdom; you simply don't know what having more would do to your heart. But God does.

Also remember that God provides the necessities of life for exactly as long as is required for him to accomplish his purposes with and in you. You can mark this down: one day, unless Jesus returns, God will withdraw from you his life-sustaining blessings, and you will die. Maybe it will be the blessing of food that he withholds, and you'll starve. Maybe it will be the blessing of a healthy heart, and you'll die of a heart attack. Maybe it will be the blessing of protection, and you'll die in an accident. Whatever the circumstances, though, none of those things means that your work in this life has been cut short; it means that your work is done. When my grandfather died some years ago, the pastor at his funeral said something that drove this truth home to me. He said, "At 11:32 last Wednesday night, God finished his work in brother Ralph and called him home." I cherished the specificity in that insight. God did not prolong my grandfather's life one second longer than was necessary. He finished his work at 11:32 p.m., and my grandfather went home at 11:32 p.m.

Here's the bottom line: God *delights* to provide for us—just not always exactly *when* and *how* and *for as long as* we might like.

Fifth, Jesus reminds us that pagans spend their lives pining after material things. They make such things the pursuit and passion of their lives. And why? Because they're missing the end of the story! They don't know or don't accept that life is about far more than the things of this world. They don't see what we as Christians see—that eternity stretches out before us and that the greatest blessings of God are to be had *there*, not here. Again, the irony is thick and devastating: if our conception of the favor of God is all about what we can get out of it in this world, then we're thinking like a pagan. And we don't have the favor of God at all.

Sixth, Jesus says that our heavenly Father knows we need these things. God not only can provide and not only delights to provide but also knows we need these things. What a wonderful expression of care for us. Our God is not distant or mechanical. He is our heavenly Father, the One who created us and made us, and so he knows we need things like food and clothing and shelter. That's not a surprise to him. In fact, God knows our needs infinitely better than we know them—which, by the way, is a good reason for us to trust him when he says no to something we *think* we need.

Seventh, Jesus reminds us that each day has enough trouble of its own. Don't try to pack two days' worth of trouble into one, he says. Jesus's point here strikes us as a little funny because it's so obviously true. Every day has plenty of trouble on its own, and anxiety or worry or discontent just pulls trouble from tomorrow into today. We wind up living two days' worth of trouble in one day. Of course, the issue with that approach is that God gives us grace to live each day one at a time, to face down each day's trouble as it comes. After all, it's *daily* bread God gives us, not *weekly* or *yearly* bread. When tomorrow gets here with all its trouble, we can be sure God will give us the grace to face it. But he's not going to do so beforehand, and if we try to live tomorrow's trouble before tomorrow gets here, we're going to be facing that trouble in our minds without the grace God will give us to face it at the appointed time.

I hope you can see how all this hangs together so beautifully. What Jesus wants for us, his favored children, is to be able to live a peacefully contented life, one that is spent in joyous pursuit of him. And the way we do that, rather than getting sucked under the waves of the cares of this world, is to realize that God has promised to take all our material needs into his own caring, loving hands. True, things may not always look or feel like we wish they did. There will be times of plenty *and* want, abundance *and* need. There will even come a point when God will withdraw his life-sustaining blessings and call us home. But then again, the fact that God's favor toward us doesn't always look rich and abundant is also kind of the point. We pursue him, we seek his kingdom, always with trust and rejoicing, because we know that the greatest of his blessings are not of this world at all.

They stretch, forever, into eternity.

7

The Blessing of Peace with God

On a hot, muggy day in July, a young university student was traveling through the German countryside on his way home from college. The man had graduated with a master's degree earlier that year and, at his father's urging, had just begun a course of study at the university's law school. It hadn't taken long, though, for him to realize he actually wasn't terribly interested in the law, and he was considering changing his course of study to something he considered far more important. Pondering these things as he rode toward home, he looked up to see that the skies above him had darkened ominously as a thunderstorm gathered. Suddenly, a lightning bolt struck the ground near him, knocking him off his horse and onto the muddy ground. As he fell, a cold fear that he was about to die seized his heart, and he cried out in terror, "Help me, St. Anne! I will become a monk!"

And so he did. Just over two weeks after making that vow—on July 17, 1505—Martin Luther presented himself to a monastery in Erfurt, Germany, and became a monk. Over the next several years, God would use Martin Luther in amazing ways, and he would become one of the most influential figures in Western history. He had a long road to travel before that would happen, though, a road that would land him in the darkest depths of despair he had ever known and a debilitating fear that the God he served hated him and wanted nothing more than to destroy him.

All his life, Luther had struggled with an abject terror of God. In his understanding, God was the Judge who had passed sentence on humanity, and the only hope humans had for salvation was to perform the works the church in Rome required—pilgrimages, the veneration of relics, masses, prayers, and confessions. If he did enough, Luther thought, perhaps he could escape the hottest flames of hell and only be forced to spend a few centuries in purgatory, where the flames were only a fraction as hot and the purpose was not to destroy but to burn away the dross of impurity so his soul could eventually be released into the bliss of heaven. One of the illustrations in his school books even depicted Jesus on a rainbow throne, a sword coming out of one ear, a flower out of the other, and the masses of humanity huddled under him waiting for his thundering verdict either for or against them.

All this terrified Luther, and becoming a monk didn't help. For years, even after he entered the monastery, Luther spent hours in his confessional chamber trying to remember every sin and oversight and mistake he'd made during the day and then racking his memory for any he might have forgotten. At one point, the priest appointed to hear his confessions finally threw up his hands in frustration and told Luther that he needed to go away and commit a sin that was actually worthy of confession!

That advice was of no use to Luther, and he began to suffer fits of terror that he called *Anfechtungen*, a feeling of horror and despair and abandonment so deep that Luther later said it would have killed him if it had lasted more than a tenth of an hour. His conscience was tormented with guilt, and he did everything he could think of to find peace with the God he imagined looked down on him in hatred. He fasted for days at a time, refused blankets during the freezing night, and lay in bed trying to convince himself, "I have done nothing wrong today." But then his conscience would turn on him and attack: "Have you fasted enough? Are you poor enough?" And so Luther would strip himself even of his meager nightclothes and lay in the icy dark, hoping that perhaps his suffering in the cold would appease God's fiery wrath.

Luther was at war with God, and what he needed more than anything in the world was to be at peace, to know that God did not in fact hate him but was pleased with him. He needed to have some confidence that God's face was toward him and not against him, that he had God's favor instead of his wrath.

In 1513, still suffering from the *Anfechtungen* and having exhausted his confessor's patience, Luther was appointed to study and teach the Bible to undergraduate students in the university. Luther was, of course, terrified that he would defile the Holy Book, but he began his studies in the Psalms. When he came to Psalm 22, he immediately recognized in the very first verse the voice of Jesus on the cross: "My God, my God, why have you forsaken me?" That cry captured Luther's imagination, and he began to meditate deeply on what it might mean. Luther clearly understood why he himself—a worm and a sinner and a rebel against God's majesty—might suffer like this, but why would the Son of God ever do so? Why would Jesus, the perfect and spotless Lamb, ever have to suffer the horror of being rejected by God? Why would Jesus have to suffer the *Anfechtungen*?

As Luther continued to study the Bible, he realized that the answer must be that Jesus was not suffering for his own sin. He didn't have any! No, the only explanation was that, as Paul put it, Christ had become sin for us. He "bore our sins in his body" (1 Pet. 2:24), he became "a curse for us" (Gal. 3:13), all so that we might become "the righteousness of God" (Rom. 3:5). So there it was, the solution to Luther's warfare with God. Because of what Jesus had done for him, Luther's sin was wiped away and he stood righteous and justified in God's sight. He was united to Jesus, with Jesus's death and righteousness credited to him, and God would now no more condemn him and cast him away than he would cast his own Son into hell. That realization caused Luther's heart to explode with joy.

> I felt myself to be reborn and to have gone through open doors into paradise. The whole of Scripture took on a new meaning, and whereas before "the justice of God" had filled me with hate, now it became to me inexpressibly sweet in

greater love. [It] became to me a gate to heaven. . . . If you have a true faith that Christ is your Savior, then at once you have a gracious God, for faith leads you in and opens up God's heart and will, that you should see pure grace and overflowing love. This it is to behold God in faith: that you should look upon his fatherly, friendly heart, in which there is no anger or ungraciousness. He who sees God as angry does not see him rightly but looks only on a curtain, as if a dark cloud had been drawn across his face.[1]

At long last and in the face of Jesus, Martin Luther had found peace with God and an end to his guilt.

Grace to You, and Peace

When the apostle Paul wrote letters to the churches he had planted, he often began them with the greeting, "Grace to you, and peace." Both *grace* and *peace* were well chosen, because they captured beautifully what Jesus won for us by his life, death, and resurrection in our place. He won grace for us—the favor of God given in spite of our rebellion against him—and the result is that now, for the first time since Adam and Eve were banished from Eden, we can be at peace with God.

The story of humanity is a story of warfare with God and separation from him. Over and over again in the Bible, God makes it clear that we as humans are not at peace with him, not welcome in his presence. Adam and Eve were banished from the garden, and an angel with a fiery sword was placed at the entryway to prevent them from going back. When God met the nation of Israel at Mount Sinai, he commanded

Moses to put barriers around the mountain to prevent the people from coming up to him. If anyone broke through the barriers, he commanded, the archers were to shoot them dead! When the temple in Jerusalem was finally built, the people were allowed only into the courtyard; they were forbidden from entering the central Holy of Holies where God dwelt, and in fact, a sixty-foot-high, thick curtain stood at the entrance to it, reminding them that they lived in a precarious cease-fire with God, not in true peace.

What an amazing moment it was, then, when that curtain was torn in two from top to bottom as Jesus died. Finally, the enmity between God and man was ended; the separation was over, and for the first time since Eden had been closed against them, human beings were invited back into the presence of God—not in dread, not for judgment and condemnation, but in peace and for celebration! That's what Paul is talking about when he says in Romans 5:1, "Therefore, since we have been justified by faith, we have peace with God through our Lord Jesus Christ."

Declared Righteous by God

The word *justified* in Romans 5:1 means "declared righteous." It's a term that comes from the courtroom, as if you stood before the throne of God and were awaiting his judgment on your life. What you need in that moment is for God to hand down the judgment, "You are righteous," rather than, "You are guilty." That's what Jesus does in the exchange that takes place between him and those who are united to him by faith. He takes our sin on himself, dies because of it, and then credits his perfect, divine-favor-winning life to us. And thus

God looks at us and what he sees is no longer our rebellion against him but rather his Son's perfect obedience credited (or "imputed") to us. And so the verdict comes down: "You are righteous! You are justified."

Now here's the beauty of all this. Once the Judge of all the universe hands down his verdict, it will never change. There is no appeal, and there is no overturning of his judgment. It's as Paul says in Romans 8:33–34:

> Who shall bring any charge against God's elect? It is God who justifies. Who is to condemn? Christ Jesus is the one who died—more than that, who was raised—who is at the right hand of God, who indeed is interceding for us.

In other words, once God has spoken, who's going to overturn his verdict? No one. After God has handed down his judgment that we who are united to Jesus are righteous, who's going to stand and condemn us anyway? No one. The throne of God is the highest court in the universe, and therefore his verdict of "righteous" wraps around our lives like a fortress of diamond. It will never be overturned.

Even more, Paul says it is Christ Jesus who has died, and who has been raised from the dead, and who now sits at the right hand of God "interceding for us." Sometimes the word *interceding* simply means "praying for" someone. Here, though, it's another legal term, and it means that Jesus advocates or argues for us like an attorney—or better, like a champion. What an incredible image! Satan the accuser stands with his crooked finger pointed at you and says, "This one has sinned and deserves to die." But Jesus rises from his throne at the right hand of God and says, "It's true.

This one has sinned, and the penalty for sin is death. I will not argue that this one is innocent. But, my Father, may it please the court to remember that I have already died for this one's sins."

I hope you can see the point. This is where any and all peace with God comes from. "*Since* we have been justified by faith," Paul says, "we have peace with God" (Rom. 5:1, emphasis added). And what a deep and cleansing and lasting peace it is.

How Louie Zamperini Found Peace

In her spectacular book *Unbroken: A World War II Story of Survival, Resilience, and Redemption*, Laura Hillenbrand tells the story of Louie Zamperini, the American Olympic runner who was shot down over the Pacific Ocean by Japanese fighters during World War II. After surviving forty-seven days stranded at sea, he and his crewmates were eventually rescued, only to spend months on end enduring the most horrifying torture and deprivation imaginable at the hands of their captors. Starved, whipped, made to stand in the scorching sun holding railroad ties above his head, even forced to watch some of his fellow captives tortured to death, Zamperini experienced nothing as horrible as the soul-crushing torment inflicted by Japanese Sergeant Mutsuhiro Watanabe, known by the prisoners simply as the Bird.

Probably because of Zamperini's own personal resolve not to bow under the torture, the Bird made it his personal mission, over months, to break the American's body and will. He singled Zamperini out for brutal beatings, lunging at him, screaming and with his fists flying, and repeatedly left Zamperini bruised and bleeding. He beat him mercilessly with a belt, the end of which held a two-inch metal buckle that once left Zamperini deaf for two weeks after crashing into his eardrum. The Bird starved the prisoners, offering them food and then abruptly rescinding the offer and sending them away. He forced them to stand all night long in the dead of winter saluting the Japanese flag and forced them illegally to perform hard labor.

Amazingly, Zamperini survived, and when the war ended, he finally made it home to his wife, Cynthia. Even so, the memories of the Bird's torment continued to torture him. Zamperini would lie awake at night, afraid of the nightmares that came without respite. He descended into alcoholism and began to hallucinate, one time even snapping out of a trance to realize he was on top of his pregnant wife, strangling her. He had thought he was strangling the Bird.

Finally, Zamperini decided there was only one way to wrest peace from his torment: he would kill the Bird. He would go to Japan, he would find Mutsuhiro Watanabe, and he would murder him. Rage consumed him, and a lust for revenge devoured his heart. He spent hours at the gym pummeling a bag and imagining it was the Bird's body he was breaking. He drank himself to drunkenness almost daily and dreamed of the day he would watch the Bird die at his hands.

One night in 1949, however, Cynthia dragged him, quite against his will, to hear an upstart preacher by the name of Billy Graham. Over two nights, Zamperini listened to Graham's message of how every person is a sinner, filled with anger and lust and the desire for revenge, and that only Jesus Christ can give forgiveness and peace. Zamperini turned to leave at the end of the service, but what Graham was saying arrested his soul. He remembered a vow he had whispered long ago as he floated in a life raft in the middle of the Pacific Ocean: "If you will save me, I will serve you forever." In that moment, he turned back toward the preacher and began walking toward a new life in Christ.

When he got home that night, Zamperini went to the kitchen and, instead of pouring himself a drink, emptied every bottle of liquor he owned down the drain. He found an old Bible, long forgotten, walked down to a park, and began to read about the Jesus who had saved him. Here's how Hillenbrand ends the account:

> Resting in the shade and the stillness, Louie felt profound peace. When he thought of his history, what resonated with him now was not all that he had suffered but the divine love that he believed had intervened to save him. He was not the worthless, broken, forsaken man that the Bird had striven to make of him. In a single, silent moment, his rage, his fear, his humiliation and helplessness, had fallen away. That morning, he believed, he was a new creation. Softly, he wept.[2]

Louie Zamperini's life would never be the same. The flashbacks and nightmares never returned, he gave up alcohol, and the rage and anger were gone for the rest of his life. His very heart was different. Now instead of a consuming desire to kill the Bird in revenge, there was forgiveness and love toward him, even a desire to meet him and communicate to him the same life-transforming news that Zamperini had heard from Billy Graham. Sadly, the meeting never happened. Watanabe refused. In the end, though, what mattered was that Louie Zamperini had been radically and forever changed. He had met Jesus, he had received the gracious favor of God, and now—at last—he was at peace.

The End of Guilt

What Louie Zamperini experienced is something available to every Christian, to every person united to Jesus the Well-Pleasing One. If you are a believer in Christ, then God is well pleased with you. You have been forgiven, justified, and declared righteous, and therefore you are at peace with God.

So many Christians, however, don't experience that sense of peace and easy friendship with God. Why is that? I'm convinced that much of the problem is that they never let themselves truly *rest* in the reality of their salvation. As much as they might tell themselves they are saved, forgiven, and even under God's gracious favor, there always remains a nagging fear that somehow it might all go away. Many times that fear is driven by a persistent feeling of guilt over past or even present sins.

But if God's favor and the peace it brings mean anything at all, they mean we as Christians no longer live under the crushing guilt of sin. In fact, sin's dominion over us—its power to do us harm and to separate us from God's favor, delight, and love—has been shattered by Jesus's work on our behalf and in our place. That's what Paul means when he says in Romans 6:6 that "our old self was crucified with him in order that the body of sin might be brought to nothing, so that we would no longer be enslaved to sin." Apart from Christ, you are a slave to the guilt and reality of your rebellion against God. Sin has its throne deep in your heart, and it coerces obedience from you no matter how hard you try to reason out of it, or feel bad about it, or even assert your will against it. And then it lashes you with crushing guilt when you obey it and bow to its demands. That's the "old self."

But Paul says that when you become a Christian—when you put your faith in Jesus and are united to him—that wretched old self is crucified and put to death. Sin's dominion is broken; its throne, even in the deepest recesses of your being, is overturned. But how? Why?

The answer comes in the next verse, Romans 6:7. Paul says that we are no longer enslaved to sin, "for the one who has died has been set free from sin." The important thing to see about this verse is that it's not just a universal truism; it's not just an axiom, as if Paul is saying that *everyone in the world* who dies is suddenly free from sin. That wouldn't even be true, after all. No, Paul is saying something much more specific. He's talking, again, about the reality of our union with Jesus. He's saying, "The one who has died *in Christ, with Christ, just as we've been talking about*, is set free from sin."

What an incredible truth. Because you have died with Christ, sin's shackles and chains are shattered. You are set free from sin and its guilt. But I want you to see one more thing. The phrase "has been set free from sin" is actually and literally "has been *justified* from sin." Do you see what Paul is saying here? It is God's justification of you, his declaration that because of Jesus you are righteous, that breaks sin's dominion over you and topples its throne. The old self is crucified and brought to nothing, the body of sin is broken and destroyed, and the enslavement of its guilt over you is ended *because you are declared by God to be innocent and righteous.*

Stand Up Again, and Live!

Here's the point: if you want to experience the peace that comes from having the favor and pleasure of God, it's crucial that you embrace the forgiveness and justification Jesus has won for you. The fact is there's no spiritual value in sitting endlessly in the guilt of sin. It's amazing, actually, that so many Christians think (sometimes without really thinking about it) we'll somehow get extra points from God for feeling really bad about sin for a really long time. But what I want you to see is that wallowing in guilt can actually perpetuate sin's enslavement of you. It can be an invitation for sin to remain on the throne of your life long after King Jesus has stripped it of its right to be there. Do you see why that is? Think about it: what is it that creates enslavement to sin in the life of someone who should be reveling in the joy of forgiveness? It's guilt—a sense of shame and self-reproach that drives out joy. Friend, Jesus has shattered sin's claims over you; if you are *in him*, then you are forgiven and clean and justified and a delight to God's eyes. But sitting interminably in this kind of guilt and self-loathing can actually lock phantom chains around your wrists and drop you back into an enslavement to sin.

I know Christians talk often about being "broken" over sin and how good that is. They come away from church services and conferences, and they talk about how good it felt to be "broken" in God's presence. They pray and sing and ask God to "break their hearts." And to a certain degree, that's fine and even good. After all, Psalm 51:17 says, "A broken and contrite heart, O God, you will not despise." But listen: a Christian is never meant to *sit* in brokenness. We are not meant to lie forever in the dirt but rather to "Rise, go, and sin no more!" In other words, when you sin as a Christian, the proper response is not to collapse in guilt, slap sin's phantom chains around your wrists again, and spend days or even weeks telling yourself how unworthy you are to have God's favor and delight. Of course you're unworthy to have God's favor! That's the whole point of the gospel! What you're meant to do, instead, is recognize your sin for what it is, agree with God that it is evil and yet another reason why you deserve to die eternally in hell, and then . . .

> turn to King Jesus,
> find forgiveness,
> let his love and resurrection life course through you like
>   sap through a branch,
> stand up again,
> and live!

Knowing that we enjoy the favor of God because of what Jesus has done for us means the warfare between us and God is ended. As the old hymn puts it so beautifully:

> Death and the curse were in my cup,
> O Christ, 'twas full for me!
> But Thou hast drained the last dark drop,
> 'Tis empty now for me!
> That bitter cup, love drank it up
> Now only blessing's left for me!
> Jehovah bade his sword awake;
> O Christ, it woke 'gainst thee!
> Thy blood the flaming blade must slake,

Thy heart its sheath must be!
All for my sake, my peace to make;
Now sleeps that sword for me![3]

When Jesus died on the cross, absorbing in his own soul and body the full punishment that our sin deserved, the cannons of God's wrath fell silent. We were—at long last—without guilt and at peace, forever, with God.

8

The Blessing of New Life

My dad called me in the middle of the night several years ago. I was groggy, and it took a moment for the message to sink in, but I finally understood. My grandfather, a wonderful Christian man, World War II veteran, cattle rancher, and die-hard Texas Rangers fan, had died of a heart attack. I remember sitting on the edge of the bed, listening to my father's broken but still strong voice telling me the news. My grandfather's death was a blow to me, because it was the first time in my life that someone very close to me had died, the first time I really had to come to grips with what death meant.

Over the next week or so, one thing I began to notice is that we try really hard to make death beautiful. At my grandfather's funeral, we sang beautiful songs, people said beautiful words, and the church building was full of hundreds of flowers whose colors tried their best to convince us it wasn't so bad. My grandfather's body was dressed in one of his favorite gray suits, a diamond tie tack glinting from his chest just like it had on a thousand Sunday mornings as he took up the offering. But, of course, in the middle of it all, there was the box—the casket in which his body lay, lifeless. The box was beautiful too, of course. Polished to a shine and trimmed in gleaming metal, it looked like it had been fashioned for something more than to be buried in the ground.

My grandfather had done a two-year tour of duty in the 447th Bomb Group of the Eighth Air Force, even at one point being shot down by enemy flak and being forced to bail out behind enemy lines. To this day, I marvel at the presence of mind he must have had, first, to dig a piece of flak out of his stricken plane, and then, after he landed on the ground, to cut a two-inch square out of his parachute and stuff both artifacts into his pocket. "I wanted to show them to my grandkids," he said. He was nineteen years old at the time. I thought of that piece of parachute as we all startled at the fifteen-gun volley fired in his honor by members of the American Legion.

Graveside services are made to look beautiful too. The giant mound of dirt dug out of the ground is covered with green turf, silk-covered chairs are placed in front of the now-closed casket, and the flowers make their appearance again. Beautiful and comforting words are spoken again, hugs and tears are exchanged, and soon the people wearing beautiful clothes climb in their cars and leave. At my grandfather's funeral, I decided not to leave. I stood there and watched as the men in overalls—not suits—came to bury my grandfather's body.

There's nothing beautiful about a burial, nothing elegant or even graceful. The workers rolled the turf off the mound of dirt and, more roughly than I expected, wrapped the casket in nylon bands. Then they began to lower the box, and the body, into the ground. It wasn't a smooth, quiet, even movement to the bottom of the hole. The casket tilted and pitched as the workers released the bands a little, then a little more. They talked to one another, not in the hushed funeral voices I'd grown used to over the past few days but in barked orders not to drop it, or to lift this corner a little more, or to lower that one. For all that, what's stuck with me all these years is the fact that the grave—either from rain the night before or the height of the water table—had filled with about six inches of water. When my grandfather's body finally settled at the bottom, the nylon bands were pulled muddy and wet out from under the casket and out of the grave, and that was the end. My grandfather was dead and buried.

The Funeral of a Friend

One of my favorite stories in the Bible is told in John 11, when Jesus himself attended a funeral that in so many ways must have been like my grandfather's. Jesus was actually in the region of Batanea, about 93 miles northeast of Jerusalem, when word came from a city called Bethany that his friend Lazarus had fallen ill and was near death. Both the messenger and the disciples expected Jesus to act immediately, to go to his friend and *do something*. After all, they knew Jesus's power. They had seen him heal people before, and they knew he could do the same this time. If his friend Lazarus was sick, surely Jesus would act immediately to heal him. Astonishingly, though,

Jesus decided to stay where he was for two more days. Why would he do that? Why would he do something that seems so callous, so unloving and uncaring? But, of course, what he did *wasn't* unloving. In fact, John is careful to say, "Now Jesus loved Martha and her sister and Lazarus. So, when he heard that Lazarus was ill, he stayed two days longer in the place where he was" (John 11:5–6). Did you catch that? The Bible says that he loved them *and therefore* he stayed. See, the town where Lazarus lived was a four-day journey from Batanea, and verse 11 says that Lazarus died two days after the messenger found Jesus. What that means is that if Jesus had left immediately upon the messenger's arrival, he wouldn't have arrived in Bethany in time to save Lazarus anyway; he'd have been two days late. Besides, Jesus had other plans entirely, plans that would allow Mary, Martha, the disciples, and all the people present to see God's power in Jesus to a degree they had never seen it before. But those plans also depended on Jesus staying put for two more days.

When the time came, Jesus departed from Batanea and made the ninety-three-mile walk to Bethany. As he drew close, Martha met him on the road to greet him. "If you had been here," she said, "my brother would not have died" (John 11:21). She wasn't rebuking him; she was simply stating what she knew to be true. Jesus could have healed him . . . if only he'd been there. Jesus responded to Martha with exquisite ambiguity. "Your brother will rise again," he said (v. 23). It's hard not to read those words with the end of the story in mind, but to Martha, it just sounded like the kind of thing one naturally says at a funeral. And she responded with equal politeness: "I know that he will rise again in the resurrection on the last day" (v. 24). In other words, "Yes,

I know. And that gives me hope. Thank you for your kind words at this difficult time."

But then Jesus said something completely unexpected. "I am the resurrection and the life. Whoever believes in me, though he die, yet shall he live, and everyone who lives and believes in me shall never die" (vv. 25–26). However you look at it, those are incredible words. It would have been mind-blowing enough for Jesus to say, "I can *give* resurrection and life." But he didn't. He said, "I *am* the resurrection and the life." And Martha believed him. In the midst of her own grief at her brother's death, she was beginning to see Jesus for who he really was—not just someone who could heal the sick and do a miracle here and there but the One who could even roll back death itself.

In our modern, sanitized, white-plastic-and-blue-LED world, we work hard to avoid being confronted with death. Our funerals are shrouded in slick beauty, and people die in hospital beds surrounded by machines far more often than they do in their homes surrounded by their grandchildren. Even our meat is packaged in such a way that we don't have to think about—much less *see*—the death that had to take place so we can eat it. But even though we try to hide from it, death still works in us in so many ways. Our bodies decay, our relationships break down, our world tends toward chaos and violence, and it all seems so unstoppable. Yet here was the man who could stop it all and even reverse it, the One who radiated life and not death. That's what he wanted Martha to believe, to trust in and rely on. And she did.

As Jesus made his way farther toward Bethany, John tells us that Mary also came out to meet him. When Jesus saw her and heard her weeping with the others who had come with her, the Bible says he "was deeply moved in his spirit" (v. 33). The phrase "deeply moved" doesn't quite do justice to the original word used there. It means something more like "indignant" or "incensed," even "furious." That's the thing about Jesus. He didn't take death as inevitable; he didn't see it in any way as a friend, or just a part of the circle of life, or the natural corollary to life. This scene of death and despair and weeping and hopelessness actually kindled *anger* in him. The way sin and death had ravaged people he loved—how it had left them grief-stricken, broken, and helpless—left the Son of God *furious*.

But, of course, the question was what he would do now. And at this point in the Bible's story, we realize that the answer on everybody's mind was, "Nothing. He's going to do nothing." At first, Jesus didn't do anything extraordinary at all. Like any mourner, he asked Mary and Martha where the tomb was, probably—at least this was what everyone would have thought—so he could have a moment of silent prayer for his friend. They offered to take him there and, again like any mourner, he wept. John 11:35 is the shortest verse in the Bible: "Jesus wept." If that's all you could see, it would be an astonishing picture of weakness—the Miracle Worker brought low by the one enemy even *he* couldn't best . . . death. That's exactly what the people thought too. "See how he loved him!" some said (v. 36). Others shook their heads at the senselessness of it all: "Could not he who opened the eyes of the blind man also have kept this man from dying?" they asked (v. 37). Yes, maybe he could have before death, they all thought. But not now.

Jesus didn't weep for long, though. After arriving at the tomb, Jesus commanded them to take the stone away from the doorway. Martha was shocked at the request. It had been four days since her brother had died, the body had started to decompose, and so there would be a pungent odor of rot and decay. Even so, the stone was removed, Jesus prayed, and then he called out in a loud voice, "Lazarus, come out" (v. 43).

It's been said that Jesus's authority over death was so absolute that if he hadn't specified Lazarus's name, every dead body in the graveyard would have come back to life. Either way, it happened just as Jesus said. The man who had been dead came out, alive. It wouldn't have been a pretty scene. Lazarus didn't come out of the tomb with his arms in the air and a triumphant smile on his face. The Bible says his hands and feet were still tied when he came out, and he had a veil over his face. So he would have come out of the tomb kind of hopping and shuffling, not strutting. But even if he looked faintly ridiculous shambling out of the grave, hell's legions knew what it meant. For all its fearsome and unbroken domination over mankind, death cowered at a word from this man's lips, and its iron grip on the throat of humanity slipped. Irrevocably.

That grip would fail entirely a few weeks later when Jesus himself would rise from the dead. Unlike Lazarus, though, Jesus wouldn't stumble out of the tomb still encumbered by the grave clothes. He would rise triumphantly, the shroud left to one side and the veil nearby. Unlike Lazarus, Jesus wouldn't just be pulled back out of death. He would go *through* it and come out victoriously on the other side. He would be resurrected with a glorified body, never to die again.

United to the Source of All Life

Resurrection was not something that merely *happened* to Jesus. Life is not something that Jesus merely *possesses* or that he simply *gives*. That's the point he was making to Martha. "I *am* the resurrection," he said. "I *am* the life." In another place, he said, "I am the way, and the truth, and the life" (John 14:6). And in another, he said, "As the Father has life in himself, so he has granted the Son also to have life in himself" (John 5:26). In other words, *life is inherent to Jesus*. It originates with him, pulses in him, and streams from him like light from a star. Wherever there is life in the universe—whether spiritual or physical—it owes its beginning and its continued existence to him. Here's what that means for us who are united to Jesus through faith and enjoy his favor and pleasure: we are irrevocably, inseparably united to the Source of all life in the universe, and there is enormous power to be found in that.

This reality is far more than just a way of thinking too. It's more than a metaphor that can help you change your attitude about life if you just meditate on it. No, the fact that you are united to the Source of life is an *objective reality* whether you're thinking about it at any given moment or not. If you are a believer, then you are grafted into, connected with, united to Jesus Christ, and his resurrection power— that power that will raise your dead body from the grave someday—is *already* at work in you bringing life to what was dead, calling into existence that which was not, and conforming you more each day to the image of Jesus. Let's consider some of the ways the life of Jesus is at work in us.

Bringing Life to What Was Dead

In Ephesians 2, Paul says that before we were united to Jesus Christ, we were "dead in our trespasses" (v. 5). We were not simply sick and in need of a doctor to make us well. We were not drowning and in need of someone to throw us a life preserver. No, we were dead, not just ill. We were dead at the bottom of the ocean, not just drowning. And just as it took a miracle of astonishing divine power to bring Lazarus's dead body back to life, so it took a miracle to bring our dead souls back to life. "God, being rich in mercy," Paul says, "because of the great love with which he loved us, even when we were dead in our trespasses, made us alive together with Christ" (Eph. 2:4–5).

You have to get your mind around what that means. Becoming a Christian isn't just a matter of turning over a new leaf, or deciding to become a better person, or making a decision that you're going to raise your children in the church. It is the result of a supernova effusion of divine energy and power that brings light out of darkness and life out of death. In talking about what it meant for Abraham to be saved, Paul put it like this: Abraham believed in the God "who gives life to the dead and calls into existence the things that do not exist" (Rom. 4:17). Do you see how he put those two phrases in parallel with each other? The power that gives life to the dead is the *same* power that called the cosmos into existence.

Dear Christian, your salvation—the fact that you now stand redeemed, forgiven, justified, and favored by God—was no small thing. The word that God spoke to your heart to awaken it to faith in Christ was no afterthought, no mere whisper. No, the divine word of life that brought you to spiritual life could have created a universe.

What's more, that same life is at work in you *now*, bringing new life where there was once only death. Maybe you need to realize anew that God actually does this kind of thing: he brings to life that which was dead. Maybe you have patches of hopelessness and death in your life, places where you've given up hope that God can or will give life again—a fight with sin, a crushing set of circumstances, a decayed relationship. If that's you, even if despair set in a long time ago, lift up your eyes to the Resurrection and the Life, the One who delights in you and to whom you are united. Let your faith in his life-giving power be renewed. God makes lives scorched by sin bloom again. He makes hearts fossilized by rebellion beat again and live again. He takes dry bones and gives them life.

I've seen the power of the resurrection bring life to so many people in so many ways during my years as a pastor. People who long ago surrendered to addiction found supernatural strength to fight. Men and women scarred by abuse saw the pain heal and the memories become evidence of God's care and love even in the worst experiences of life. Wastelands and deserts of greed, lust, anger, and hatred heard the voice of the Resurrection and the Life and bloomed into gardens of love, joy, peace, patience, kindness, goodness, faithfulness, gentleness, and self-control. That's what the resurrection power of Jesus does: it flows like a river into the deserts of your life and makes them live.

One sweet woman who was a member of my church for several years tells the story of how, during the birth of her first daughter, she suffered complications during the birth process that almost led to her death. It was a touch-and-go situation for days on end, including emergency surgery to try to correct a very dangerous problem. For years afterward, this sister says she struggled with the fear and dread of the memory of those days, even to the point that she was afraid to have more children. What if it happens again? she wondered. For a time, the fear became almost debilitating and created a deep dread and even depression in her heart. But she was also a Christian, under the favor and delight of God and united to the Source of all life. And over time, as she tells the story, "God slowly rewrote those memories in my mind and heart. Instead of seeing only a black hole of fear and despair, I came to recognize God's hand in those experiences. They became trophies of God's grace to me, monuments to what he is able to do and how he is able to care for us even in the darkest times." The transformation—the "rewriting"—of those memories wasn't fast for her, but it was real and lasting. Like the living sap of a tree making a fruitless branch bloom once more, those memories of death became testimonies of life.

Where is the death in your life? Hold it out to him, and let him call it into life. Let him call into existence again that which long ago ceased to be. Do you believe he can do that kind of work? That's what Jesus asked Martha: "I am the resurrection and the life," he said. "Do you believe this?" Martha did. How about you?

The Death of Death

One of the most difficult parts of being a parent is seeing your children afraid and not being able to help them or alleviate the fear. Sometimes a hug or a snuggle or a night spent sleeping in Mom and Dad's bed takes care of the fear. But sometimes it doesn't, and the fear persists and even becomes debilitating. More than a few times in my years as a pastor, I've talked with people—both children and adults—for whom death is a fearsome and terrifying enemy. It's not a surprising fear. Death seems so inescapable and so final. It is merciless, tearing families apart, cruelly taking away the ones we love sometimes with no warning.

But the beauty of being united to Jesus, of living under his delight and favor, is that death no longer has any authority over us. "I have the keys of Death and Hades," Jesus said (Rev. 1:18). In other words, he conquered death; he defeated it. As I told my own son when he was terrified of death, that doesn't mean Jesus just defeated it nicely either, like in a game of chess. No, he kicked death in the teeth! He chained it and owns it, and it does nothing apart from his command. Which means that now the only authority death has over you is the authority King Jesus has *chosen* to give it. Do you know what that is? Do you know what authority Jesus has given death over you? One thing and one thing only: to deliver you safely into his arms when it's time for you to go home.

What's more, even that limited bit of authority will not last forever. Paul promises in 1 Corinthians 15:26 that when Jesus comes back to destroy his enemies and set the world right, the last enemy to be destroyed will be death itself. Death will watch as all its work through the centuries is reversed, and every one of the bodies it laid in the ground is raised to new life, some to judgment and some to reward. And then, when all its work is undone and overturned, death will die at the hands of King Jesus the Resurrected. And all his beloved children—who suffered so deeply at death's hands—will rejoice at its end.

I cried on the day of my grandfather's funeral. I cried when they fired the salute, and I cried when they gave the flag to my grandmother. I cry still sometimes when I remember him. But none of what I saw that day—the grave, my grandfather's casket splashing into the mud—causes me to despair or fear. And I know in my heart that even at the moment of his death, it didn't cause him to despair either. Why? Because he was a Christian. Yes, my grandfather died, but I hope that when the moment came he remembered the promise of 1 Corinthians 15:

> Then comes the end, when he delivers the kingdom to God the Father after destroying every rule and every authority and power. For he must reign until he has put all his enemies under his feet. The last enemy to be destroyed is death. . . . I tell you this, brothers: flesh and blood cannot inherit the kingdom of God, nor does the perishable inherit the imperishable. Behold! I tell you a mystery. We shall not all sleep, but we shall all be changed, in a moment, in the twinkling of an eye, at the last trumpet. For the trumpet will sound, and the dead will be raised imperishable, and we shall be changed. For this perishable body must put on the imperishable, and this mortal body must put on immortality. When the perishable puts on the imperishable, and the mortal puts on immortality, then shall come to pass the saying that is written:
> "Death is swallowed up in victory."
> "O death, where is your victory?
> O death, where is your sting?"
> The sting of death is sin, and the power of sin is the law. But thanks be to God, who gives us the victory through our Lord Jesus Christ. (vv. 24–26, 50–57)

What a beautiful, life-giving, fear-eviscerating promise! One day soon, death's victory will be taken away from it, and its sting will be extracted from the heart of every one of Jesus's favored ones. And then Jesus will destroy it forever.

So yeah, I hope that on the night he died my grandfather looked death in the eye and said, "Yes, you can take me, but you and I both know that the only thing the King will allow you to do is deliver me into his arms. Oh, and death? One last thing before we go. Your own day is coming soon."

9

Fighting as Favored Sons and Daughters of the King

For fifteen years now, I've been trying to convince my wife, Moriah, that *The Lion King* is one of the best movies of all time. I know I should be embarrassed by that opinion, but I've decided I don't care what anyone thinks of me because of it. I love *The Lion King*, and I'm not backing down.

On our very first date together, Moriah asked me over dinner what my favorite movie was. I could have said a lot of things in that moment. I could have wowed her with my sophistication by saying *Casablanca* or *Citizen Kane*. I could have subtly tied myself to courageous warriors of old by saying *Braveheart* or *The Patriot*. I could have pandered shamelessly by saying *It's a Wonderful Life* or *Gone with the Wind*. But I did none of those things. Instead, I went for honesty.

"I think, probably, *The Lion King*," I said.

Moriah nodded silently and changed the subject. She told me after we got married that she nearly called the whole thing off right then and there.

But that's fine. She married me anyway, so she's stuck with me now—and my movie choices—and now I've been engaged in a decade-and-a-half-long mission to convince her of *The Lion King*'s genius. If I ever get through to her, I have a feeling it's going to be because of one particular scene—the one in which the young lion prince Simba realizes anew who he really is and finally decides to do what is necessary to claim his rightful place and identity as king of the tribe.

The scene opens with Simba almost in tears after an argument with his friend Nala, who had been pressing on Simba his responsibility to return to Pride Rock and depose his uncle Scar, who had usurped the throne after murdering Simba's father, King Mufasa. (If you don't understand all those references, that's probably because you haven't seen the movie, and, well, shame on you. Shame.) Anyway, at the end of the argument, Simba walks away and says, "She's wrong. I can't go back." Suddenly, he hears the sounds of chanting coming from a tree behind him. It's the old monkey Rafiki singing a lighthearted ditty about squashed bananas—hardly good background music for Simba's self-pitying reverie. Simba tries to shoo Rafiki away, but the monkey persists, and Simba gets more and more annoyed as he tries to get away.

"Creepy little monkey," Simba says. "Will you stop following me? Who *are* you?"

Rafiki swings around in front of Simba to block his escape and puts his nose right in the lion's face. "The question is, *Whooo* . . . are you?"

Startled by the question, and then saddened, Simba sighs and answers, "I thought I knew. Now I'm not so sure."

"Well, *I* know who you are," the monkey says. "Shh. Come here. It's a secret." He grabs Simba's ear and pulls it close, and something in Simba's face tells us he's beginning to think that maybe this baboon really does know something about him—a secret about his identity. But just as Rafiki looks as though he's about to tell Simba the secret, he dances away, singing again about squashed bananas.

Frustrated, Simba shakes his head. "Enough already! What's that supposed to mean anyway?"

Rafiki seems to ponder the question for a split second, then answers, "It means you're a baboon—and I'm not!" He laughs maniacally, and Simba sighs again and shakes his head, disappointed to realize that maybe Rafiki is simply crazy.

"I think . . . you're a little confused," Simba says, turning away.

Suddenly, Rafiki's bony finger pushes against Simba's nose. "*Wrong!*" he says. "I'm not the one who's confused. You don't even know *who* you are." Over the next several minutes, the monkey reminds Simba of his identity and his destiny. He leads him to look at his own reflection in a stream, and when Simba looks, he sees something he didn't expect—not a fearful, broken lion cub but the reflection of his father, the king. "You see?" Rafiki says urgently. "He lives *in you*." The reflection is blown away as a wind sweeps across the stream, and as Simba looks into the starry sky, he sees an image of his father forming in the clouds.

"Simba," the image says.

"Father?"

"Simba, you have forgotten me."

Awestruck and horrified, Simba refuses to accept it. "No!" he says. "How could I?"

"You have forgotten who you are and so have forgotten me. Look inside yourself, Simba. You are more than what you have become. Remember who you are. You are my son and the one true king." Simba shrinks back at the words, his heart a mixture of fear and awe and sadness. But we can see something else in his face too, something that hasn't been there before—royalty. It will take some time for him to develop and grow, but Simba has remembered who he really is, and that realization has changed him forever.[1]

Remember Whose You Are

Maybe one of the reasons I love that scene so much is because the key line of it—"Remember who you are"—echos so closely something my grandmother used to say to me throughout my teenage years. Before my friends and I would pile into our cars to go to a movie, or grab dinner, or just go someplace to hang out on a weekend night, my grandmother would often hug me, look me in the eye, and say, "Have a good time. And remember whose you are."

Remember *whose* you are. I was never quite sure what she meant by that—if I was supposed to remember I was my father's son, or her grandson, or the bearer of our family name. But I've come to believe over the years that even though she never said it directly, she actually meant more than any of those things. Most of all, she meant I was a Christian—I belonged to Jesus—and therefore I should act accordingly. "You are a son of the King," my grandmother was saying. "Remember *whose* you are, and live like it."

If you think about it, our goal in this book has really been to explore together who we are as Christians. And what we've learned above all is that *who* we are is really entirely dependent on *whose* we are. In ourselves, we are rebels against God, sinners who have forfeited his favor, earned his wrath, and are deserving of nothing but an eternity of hell and separation from him and his joy. But the good news is that God's favor has now been earned by someone else—a Champion who lived every moment of his life *exactly* as God intended and won all the blessings of eternity. And even better, that Champion also exhausted in his own body, by his death on the cross, the curse that hung over us because of our rebellion. So now all the blessings of salvation that he won and owns by right—justification, sanctification, glorification, eternal life—spill down onto us because we are united to him by faith. What glorious good news!

But those aren't just sterile theological truths that you talk about in Sunday school and then lay to the side. They actually define *whose* you are and therefore *who* you are. And that in turn determines how you walk through this life, its struggles and glories, its ups and downs, its pleasures and pains. It also determines how you face down sin in your life. The fact is if all this is true of you—if you're a Christian—then you don't need to face the world or your own sin with timidity and fear. All of a sudden, you're empowered to stand up to it all square-shouldered, with the confidence of knowing that you fight and live not as a broken and shamed rebel against God but as a loved and cherished and favored child of the King.

This Means War

If you've been a Christian for very long at all, you know that living the Christian life faithfully is no easy task. Circumstances press on you from outside, your own sin and weakness assault you from within your own heart, and sometimes it's all you can do to keep putting one foot in front of the other—much less stride into the battle as a son or daughter of the King.

And let's be honest: the Christian life really is a battle from start to finish. In fact, to be a Christian is to declare war against sin until you breathe your last breath. It's what you sign up for when you bow your knee to Jesus in faith and pledge allegiance to him as your King. To do that is nothing less than to take sides in a war that has been raging in the universe since Satan rebelled against God's throne and crown. To declare yourself a Christian is to plant your flag in the ground and say, "I have a new King, and therefore I'm declaring war against Satan and against the remnants of his dominion that still exist in me." And when you do that—when you declare war against sin and hell—you can be sure that all hell declares war right back.

That's why the Christian life is no yellow brick road to heaven and why becoming a Christian doesn't mean—for any of us—that you just effortlessly start living a holy and righteous life. No, the Bible says that even after you become a Christian, sin still lives in you. The trouble is that, united to Jesus by faith, you are no longer its ally. You are no longer under its dominion and shackled by its chains but rather in open rebellion against it. And so sin turns every weapon in its arsenal against you in an effort to destroy your soul.

That's the nature of the enemy you fight: the sin that still lives in your redeemed heart would drag your soul to hell if it could. Of course, King Jesus will never let it do that—"No one will snatch them out of my hand," he said (John 10:28)—but even if it cannot destroy you entirely, sin will still be relentless in its efforts to cut you off from the joy and life of your salvation, make you useless in God's service, and wound you so badly and bury you so deeply that you waste your life in misery when you should be spending it gloriously in God's service.

That's the war we fight as Christians, and if we're honest, we should admit that apart from knowing who we are in Christ, the war would be a terrifying one. It would be quite enough to know that the world around us stands against us. But to know that even *our own hearts* are looking for an opportunity to betray us, to know that the battle rages not just all around us but *within* us, is enough to make us want to cower in fear.

Except for one thing. We fight this battle now as favored sons and daughters of the King.

Sons and Daughters of the King

That's the amazing truth we've been discovering together through this entire book. But there's one biblical passage in particular that unveils this reality in an awesome way. In Galatians 4:4–5, Paul writes, "When the fullness of time had come, God sent forth his Son, born of woman, born under the law, to redeem those who were under the law, so that we might receive adoption as sons." There are a lot of words in those verses, but do you see the point they finally come to? When he lived and died and rose again in our place, Jesus won far more for us than just a cold acquittal from the Judge of all the earth. God's favor toward us is far more than just a disinterested judicial declaration. The Bible says that because of what Jesus did for us, God has given us the gift of *adoption*.

Adoption as sons. Adoption as daughters. Without a doubt, this is one of the most mind-blowing, heart-galvanizing, courage-giving things God does when he saves us from our sin. Think about it: it would have been possible for God simply to have saved us from the curse of our sin, judicially declared us righteous, and then patted us on the back and sent us on our way—like a child who fell in the dirt and needed to be cleaned up. He could even have given us the gift of spiritual life and created a renewed earth for our pleasure. He could have reigned over us in perfect joy and righteousness and peace. And if he had done all those things, he would have been worthy of enormous praise. But he didn't leave it at that. Yes, he redeemed us, saved us, justified us, and gave us spiritual life and the promise of a renewed cosmos, but then—above and beyond anything we could have imagined— he adopted us as his own, made us his children, and brought us into the most intimate relationship with him imaginable. Not only so, but he also declared that the inheritance and reward that belonged to his Son, Jesus, by right would also be *our* inheritance. We would be not just his people but his sons and daughters. No wonder John cries out, "See what kind of love the Father has given to us, that we should be called children of God!" (1 John 3:1).

To have God's favor poured out on us—to have him turn his face toward us in delight instead of away from us in wrath—is the most profound and glorious change that can ever happen to a person. Look at these two verses that describe the difference. Ephesians 2:3 says that before we were united to Jesus, "We all once lived in the passions of our flesh, carrying out the desires of the body and the mind, and were by nature children of wrath." But John 1:12 says, "But to all who did receive [Jesus], who believed in his name, he gave the right to become children of God."

What an amazing change! Before we trust in Jesus, we are *children of wrath*. But when Jesus stands in our place, exhausts the curse, and wins God's favor, we are made *children of God*—adopted into his family forever and made heirs of everything Jesus won by his life, death, and resurrection. By now you can probably see how this happens. We are not sons and daughters of God by right; we didn't do anything to earn the reward of God's favor. No, *Jesus* is the Son of God, but when we put our faith in him, when we rely on him to save us, we are irrevocably united to him. What is his becomes ours. And because he is God's Son, that status becomes ours as well. We are not children of God by right. We did not earn that glorious status. We are children of God by union with Jesus.

The Glories of Adoption

All this—that God has adopted us as his children because of Jesus and now looks on us with the favor of a loving Father—is a fathomless well of peace and joy and security. Here are a few of its glories in which you can rest and rejoice.

First, remember that your relationship with God is sweetly intimate. To be adopted into a family is not to be hired as a

157

servant. It's not to be conscripted as a soldier. It's not even to be a welcomed, but temporary, visitor. It's to be embraced as a child, loved as a son or daughter of the Father. So many Christians could benefit greatly by meditating for a while on that truth, because they tend to think of God as a kind of parole officer who spends his days tut-tutting them from the throne and keeping a "permanent record" in heaven of all the things they do wrong or don't do well enough. And as a result, not surprisingly, they find it easy to respect and fear God but incredibly difficult to *love* him—at least in the sweet and intimate way a child loves a father. But listen carefully: the Bible does *not* present God as a parole officer or a prison guard or a disciplinarian or an accuser. It shows us that he is a loving, compassionate, yearning, protecting *Father*. That's why the Bible says several times that we cry out to God with the words, "Abba! Father!" *Abba* is a beautiful word, full of sweet intimacy. It's the kind of easily pronounced word a toddler uses to address their father, something like Dada. It's full of affection and tenderness, and yet we are invited to use it to address the God of the universe.

Second, your relationship with God as his son or daughter will never change. Through all the ages of eternity, nothing can shake or alter or call into question your identity as a child of God. Why? You already know the answer. Our status as sons and daughters comes only because we are united to Christ, and nothing will ever change Jesus's status and identity as the Son of God. Our status as sons and daughters of God is simply not dependent on us. Now that's not to say we cannot displease our Father. Of course, we can, and he disciplines us sometimes. But even in those times of displeasure and discipline, the Father-child relationship doesn't change. We are always God's children, and therefore his heart is always full of love for us. He always looks at us as sons and daughters, even when he is displeased with us.

I have three children who—believe it or not—sometimes require discipline. One of them, the middle one, used to have the most abject look of terror on his face when I would correct him about something. The scene probably did cut a pretty stern picture. My face was full of displeasure as I looked at him, and he was rocking back a bit on his heels with his eyes wide open and his lips turned down in that way kids look when they're about to cry. But as stern as the picture might have looked from the outside, on the inside those were the moments when—looking into his scared little face—I was most bursting with love for the little guy. Yes, in one sense, our relationship and joy had been disrupted by whatever he had done, and they needed to be restored by discipline, repentance, and forgiveness. But in a far more profound sense, the relationship we shared as father and son was never even *touched* by his sin. The little fellow was and always would be my beloved son, in whom I am well pleased, regardless of what might happen. So you see? If that's true in a very imperfect way between me and my children, how much more true must it be between the never-changing God and the people for whom his beloved Son died.

Third, your relationship with God means God knows you, understands you, loves you, and cares for you. One of our most self-centered laments as human beings is the hopeless complaint, "Nobody understands what I'm going through!" Well, you can be rock-solid confident that *God* does. Because of Jesus, you are his son, his daughter, his child, and far more important and fundamental than the fact that you now know

God is that God knows you. He knows who you are, what you're all about, what makes you tick, and what makes you stop ticking. He knows your sins, your dreams, your fears, your goals, and your motivations. He knows it all. That thought can be scary when you first consider it—to think that someone has such exhaustive knowledge about you! But really, it's not scary at all, because it's knowledge that's held by the One who loves you dearly, so much so that he gave his only Son for you so that you might live and not be shamed and destroyed. If that's true, then how do you imagine he's going to use that exhaustively detailed knowledge of you? To blackmail you? To shame you? To make you miserable? To reveal it all at the end of time in order to embarrass you? No. He's going to use it to help you, to push you on, to bring you to maturity, to teach you how to love him, trust him, and rejoice in him more.

Have you ever noticed how circumstances—especially the hard ones—often seem so tailor-made to press you in exactly the areas of life where your trust and love for God most need strengthening? So you begin to take something for granted . . . and God takes it away. You begin to worship something . . . and God shows you its emptiness. You begin to think too highly of yourself . . . and God brings you low. Sometimes when the circumstances of life press in on us, we want to cry out to heaven, "Why me, Lord?" Well, dear son or daughter of God, take a moment to consider this: it may well be that your hard circumstances are custom-ordained by your Father the King so that you will take another step forward in growing as a Christian. You are intimately and deeply known, and you are intimately and deeply loved.

Fourth, all the chains and claims of your former slave master are broken, and you belong to God. According to

Galatians 4:8, "Formerly, when you did not know God, you were enslaved to those that by nature are not gods." "Formerly!" Paul says. But not any longer. No longer are you enslaved to sin. No longer do you wear the chains of guilt and shame. No longer do greed and lust and anger and pride own your heart and mind. Now you belong to another—not another master but a Father—and he is fiercely jealous for you. And therefore, like a father who has redeemed and rescued his child from slavery, he will not for a moment put up with any other master—sin or law or idols—trying to make a claim on your life. "After all I have done to break those chains," he would say, "you would *dare* make a claim to enslave my child again?" Christian, you do not belong to sin any longer. You belong to your Father.

Of course, the biggest trouble is not that sin or law or idols try to drag us back to slavery. Oh, they do try, to be sure. But the biggest trouble is that our own hearts are so often willing to help them do it! We are simply *full* of foolish excuses and lies that put us back in the chains our Father broke off. "I can't beat this sin," we tell ourselves. "It's just hopeless, so why even try?" And then, consciously or not, that defeatist mind-set becomes a matter of identity to us. "I'm an angry person," we say. "I'm a lustful person. I'm a coward. I'm a glutton. I'm an addict or a greedy person or a lazy person, and that will never change. It's just who I am." But no. If we are a Christian, then we are most certainly *not* those things. Yes, of course, we still fall into those sins sometimes, all of them. But they do not define us. We are not slaves to them like we used to be, and that change of status—that change of identity—makes all the difference in the world.

Frederick Douglass was a famous abolitionist during the Civil War era who wrote powerfully about the evils of slavery and the joy of freedom. This is what he wrote:

> I have found that, to make a contented slave, it is necessary to make a thoughtless one. It is necessary to darken his moral and mental vision, and as far as possible to annihilate the power of reason. He must be able to detect no inconsistencies in slavery. He must be made to feel that his slavery is right![2]

That is precisely Satan's strategy with us as children of God. He cannot have us, but he can break us. And so he whispers, constantly, "You are a slave, and that will never change. Your slavery is right and unbreakable." Dear Christian, wake up, rise, and cast Satan and his lies back to hell. Remember whose you are. You are a child of the King.

Fifth, remember that even though the Christian life is a fight from start to finish, you fight as a Spirit-filled son or daughter of God. The apostle Paul says that the nature of that fight is to "put to death" everything in you that is sinful (Col. 3:5). That's your mission. Your struggle with sin in this life is not an arm wrestling match. It's a brutal, gladiatorial fight to the death. But here's the glorious good news in all this: as a son or daughter of God, you don't fight this battle alone. Look at what the Bible says in Galatians 4:6: "Because you are sons, God has sent the Spirit of his Son into our hearts." He's talking about the Holy Spirit, and it is by his power that you fight this battle against sin and work to put it to death. So you see? Your fight against sin—your ongoing battle to execute it—is not just a matter of strapping on your moral boots, slapping some ethical ammo around your chest, and getting after it. No, you fight now, as a son or daughter of God, with an insanely powerful partner—the Holy Spirit of God.

Older English Bibles used to refer to the Holy Spirit as the Holy Ghost. To me, that phrasing is most unfortunate, because how many of us really want to be friends with a ghost? Nobody, and what's more, it's really hard for us to get our minds around the idea that a ghost would *love* us, much less that we should feel affection for one. But the Bible actually presents the Holy Spirit not as some disembodied poltergeist but as our closest partner and fellow warrior in the fight of our lives, the One who is with us through thick and thin, crying out through the acrid smoke of the battle that we really are children of God!

Here's a question for you: Do you ever have feelings of affection for the Holy Spirit the way you do for the Son or the Father? You should. After all, it is he—the Holy Spirit—who gives you spiritual life, who brings your dead soul to life, and who unites you to Jesus. It's the Holy Spirit who will deliver your redeemed soul to Jesus on the day you breathe your last breath, and it is the Spirit who will reunite your soul with your body in the resurrection on the last day. And until then, it is the Spirit who is with you and in you and beside you—a lifeline to the age to come—constantly strengthening you, encouraging you, pouring out the love of God in your heart, crying out with you to heaven, and praying to the Father for your protection and good. What a precious relationship you have with the Holy Spirit of God.

My children will never realize, until they have their own, how much my life is interwoven and intertwined with theirs and how that leads me to love them with my whole heart.

So it is with the Holy Spirit and the children of God. His is the first voice you heard when you were called to spiritual life, and his is the first face you will see when he breathes the breath of resurrection into your lungs on the last day. And in the meantime, through all the heartbreak and joy and storms and celebrations of life, he walks with you—encouraging you, loving you, and standing shoulder to shoulder with you in the fight.

The Holy Spirit's Warfare against Sin

But how does the Holy Spirit fight with us? The Bible says that the Holy Spirit's warfare against sin in us takes two forms. He does two things that we ourselves cannot do. First, he causes the fruit of the Spirit to grow in us. The fact is we simply can't make love, joy, peace, and all the rest of the fruit grow in our lives. Oh, we can *pretend* to do so; we can *act* in a way that *looks* loving, even when our hearts are full of irritation. We can *appear* peaceful when our hearts are really chock-full of fear and turmoil. But those aren't real fruit. That's like duct taping a banana onto a tree.

No, only the Holy Spirit can cause the true fruit of godliness to grow in our lives. That's why it's called the fruit of the *Spirit*, after all. If our lives are going to bloom in love and joy and peace and patience, it's going to be because of the Holy Spirit's work. But how does this help us in the fight against sin? Think of it like this: the fruit of the Spirit is not just beautiful; it is also poisonous to sin. It crowds sin out and makes it more difficult for the fruit of sin to grow. If the Spirit has caused the fruit of love to fill up our lives, it is more difficult for hatred to grow. If our lives are full of peace, it is more difficult for turmoil and panic to find a foothold. That's one way the Spirit fights with us.

The second way, though, is that the Spirit goes to work in us, grinding and burning out the root of sin that still exists deep in our hearts, slowly but surely weakening it and destroying it. Several years ago, a tree in my backyard came down with a fatal case of a nasty disease called verticillium wilt. Without going into too much detail—you really wouldn't want to know—the tree died, and we had to have it cut down. I watched the entire process as it happened, the loggers hanging in the upper branches and cutting them down one by one, and then the trunk itself being cut down about three feet at a time. The most fascinating part of the job, though, was when they brought in a terrifying-looking machine that went to work on the stump. As the spinning blade made contact, the machine shook and shuddered, but wood chips flew everywhere and smoke started to rise, and little by little the stump was chewed to bits, burned and scorched and mauled out of existence. It didn't stand a chance.

I think it must look something like that when the Holy Spirit goes to work on the root of sin in our lives. It's not pretty, and it's not elegant, but the stump of sin ultimately doesn't stand a chance. The Holy Spirit grinds and mauls it to its roots, and over time sin's power over us becomes weaker and weaker.

That's an incredible image, isn't it? But be careful: what we're talking about here isn't just a "let go and let God" thing. We are not passive in this fight against sin, just sitting back and applauding the Spirit as he works. No, as the Spirit is grinding out the root of sin and giving life to the fruit of the Spirit, he is also freeing us and strengthening us to fight as well. That's why Romans 8:13 says that we have an obligation to "by the Spirit . . . put to death the deeds of the body," by which it means every stronghold of sin in our lives.

Our Warfare against Sin

So how do we do that? What does it mean to fight sin not as a conscripted soldier or a slave but as a Spirit-filled, favored son or daughter of God?

First, we find and embrace forgiveness and joy in Christ. Does it surprise you that this is step one? So many Christians seem to operate under a logic that says, "First I'll beat sin in my life, and *then* I'll go to Jesus for forgiveness and joy." But that logic is exactly backward. After all, it's the knowledge that we have God's favor, that we are his sons and daughters, that gives us the power and strength to fight sin in the first place. If we try to fight sin in our own strength *so that God will favor us*, we'll not only fail but also misunderstand entirely what it means to be a Christian. No, when sin raises its head in our lives, when we fall to its attacks, we go to Jesus first. We find the sweet comfort of forgiveness, remind ourselves that we are favored sons and daughters of God, and then rise and turn to battle.

Second, when we identify sin in our lives, we convict it. Declare it guilty. Drag it before the law of God, and act as judge against it before our own minds and souls. Bring Scripture to bear against it. Show ourselves why it is so evil, and remind ourselves what its goals and ends are—to destroy us. Even more, we drag it before the throne of grace and declare why that sin in particular is a betrayal of Jesus. The fact is, until we stand with Jesus in heaven, sin will sometimes defeat us;

we will even sometimes find ourselves allying with it. But once the Spirit convicts us of it, we should never take its side against our God and Savior. We should turn on it in wrath, convict it, and declare our own judgment that it is wrong and worthy of being put to death in our lives.

Third, we cultivate a longing for sin's death. Once we've seen and declared it is evil, we pray that the Holy Spirit will make us desire to be free of it, to hate it, to want to see it executed and dead and cast out of our lives. Here's the reality: as long as we cherish sin and pity it, we'll defend it, or at least we'll pull our punches so as not to wound it too badly. We'll cringe away from delivering the deathblow, and sin will continue to live and torment us. Instead, we must pray that the Spirit will make us hate it and want it to die.

Fourth, we give some serious thought to understanding how sin works in our lives. Where does it seem to get its foothold? What kinds of circumstances and situations tend to bring it out? The point here is not that we have to understand everything about our sin and its origins; in fact, if we try to do that, we'll get sucked into a bewildering vortex. In the end, sin is fundamentally irrational, and we'll never find a completely satisfying reason for it. No, the point is simply to understand sin's strategies for attacking us and learn to be on guard against them.

Fifth, we attack sin hard as soon as it pokes its head out of the ground. We don't wait until it's towering over us and breathing fire. It's easy to make that mistake, isn't it—to think, "Oh, that's just one harmless thought" or "I'll just indulge sin this much but stop before it gets too far"? Listen carefully: those are deadly mistakes. The desire of every sin, no matter how small, is to push us all the way to the end.

Every lustful thought, if it could, would become full-blown adultery if we allowed it to. Every covetous desire would become full-blown oppression. Every unbelieving thought would become atheism, and every angry reaction would become murder. That's why it is so important to grab sin and destroy it as soon as it pokes its spiky head out of the ground. We must not tolerate it or coddle it. We must bring Scripture to bear, close off its opportunity, remind ourselves of the gospel, and fight like sons and daughters of God.

Finally, we are careful not to call off the fight when sin retreats. There will be times in our lives when sin will crawl back into the ground, and the temptation will be for us as Christians to think the fight is over. But, of course, it's not. Sin is insidious in its efforts to destroy us, and many times its retreats are simply a way of putting us off guard, lulling us to sleep, and setting us up for another assault. So what do we do in those times when the temptation to sin lessens? We don't let down our guard. We continue to watch for sin's strategies and to keep the gates of our hearts closed against it. Most of all, we cultivate the fruit of the Spirit that will be poisonous to that particular sin. Do we struggle with greed? Then we pray that the Holy Spirit will teach us to be thankful and generous. Is it anger that attacks us? We ask the Spirit to teach us to trust God and his sovereignty. Are we discontent with our circumstances? We pray that we will deepen in trust and humility. Specifically, we make the environment of our lives toxic to sin.

Here's the point: from the moment God gives us spiritual life and unites us to Jesus, we are locked in a battle to the death with sin. That's just the nature of what it means to be a Christian. It's not a short battle either, or one that requires a singular enormous effort and then nothing more. No, the battle to put sin to death is one that continues until the day we stand with Jesus, and it is hard work. That's why the Bible says we are actually about the work of crucifying sin in our lives (Rom. 8:13; Gal. 5:24; Col. 3:5). That's a powerful and helpful image. One Christian described the work of crucifying sin like this:

> Crucifixion produced death not suddenly but gradually. . . . True Christians do not succeed in completely destroying sin while here below; but they have fixed it to the cross, and they are determined to keep it there till it expires.[3]

Fight as a Favored Child of the King

What an epic adventure this Christian life is. No, it's not an easy road, but Jesus never told us it would be. In fact, he told us exactly the opposite: "In the world you will have tribulation," he said. Yet then there was this: "But take heart; I have overcome the world!" (John 16:33). I hope you can see the beauty of all we've been discovering together. It's not the kind of false, plastic beauty that doesn't recognize the pain and struggle of this life. We *do* struggle, and really we shouldn't expect anything else as those who are united to Jesus the Crucified. But even in the midst of the struggle, we know that we fight as sons and daughters of God who are favored and loved by our Father. What's more, the entire Trinity—Father, Son, and Spirit—has devoted himself to our good, to seeing us safely through until we arrive at home.

If you are a Christian, know and revel in the fact that you are dearly loved and deeply cared for. After all, in heaven right now stands Jesus the King—the One who lived for you and died for you, the One to whom you are forever united—and he intercedes for you, defending you against every charge Satan might fling at you on the last day. On the throne sits God the Father, the One who loves you from all eternity and now pours out his favor on you because of what his Son has done on your behalf—not the cheap favor of money and earthly pleasure but the everlasting, infinitely valuable favor of eternity. And down here, right now, in the midst of it all, is another—the Holy Spirit—who is with you and in you every step of the way, praying for you and strengthening you and encouraging you until you are glorified on the last day.

Dear Christian, do not live this life or fight this battle as a broken, shamed slave.

Remember who you are.

Remember *whose* you are.

You live as one who bears the favor of God. You fight as a favored, well-pleasing child of the King.

NOTES

Introduction

1. C. S. Lewis, *The Weight of Glory* (New York: HarperCollins, 2001), 76.

Chapter 1 What Is the Favor of God?

1. Anne R. Cousin, "The Sands of Time Are Sinking" (Public domain, 1924). Music by Chretien Urhan.

Chapter 4 Jesus, the Winner of God's Favor

1. Robert Uhlig, "How Edmund Hillary Conquered Everest," *The Telegraph*, January 12, 2008, http://www.telegraph.co.uk/news/uknews /1575348/How-Edmund-Hillary-conquered-Everest.html.

2. Dennis McLellan, "Edmund Hillary, First to Climb Mt. Everest, Dies," *Los Angeles Times*, January 11, 2008, http://www.latimes.com /local/obituaries/la-me-hillary11jan11-story.html.

3. J. L. Reynolds, "Church Polity or the Kingdom of Christ (1899)," in *Polity: Biblical Arguments on How to Conduct Church Life (A Collection of Historic Baptist Documents)*, ed. Mark Dever (Washington, DC: Center for Church Reform, 2001), 298.

Chapter 7 The Blessing of Peace with God

1. Roland H. Bainton, *Here I Stand: A Life of Martin Luther* (Peabody, MA: Hendrickson Publishers, 2009), 48.

2. Laura Hillenbrand, *Unbroken: A World War II Story of Survival, Resilience, and Redemption* (New York: Random House, 2014), 376.

3. Anne R. Cousin, "O Christ, What Burdens Bowed Thy Head" (Public domain). Music by Ira P. Sankey.

Chapter 9 Fighting as Favored Sons and Daughters of the King

1. Roger Allers and Rob Minkoff, *The Lion King* (Burbank, CA: Walt Disney Pictures, 1994).

2. Frederick Douglass, *Narrative of the Life of Frederick Douglass, An American Slave* (Harvard, MA: Harvard University Press, 2009), 99.

3. John Stott, *The Message of Galatians* (Downers Grove, IL: Inter-Varsity, 1984), 151.

Greg Gilbert (MDiv, Southern Seminary) is senior pastor of Third Avenue Baptist Church in downtown Louisville, Kentucky. He lives in Kentucky with his wife, Moriah, and their three children, where he enjoys basketball, coffee, and Thai food.